MW01291331

POSITIVE BEHAVIOR SUPPORT PLAN TEMPLATES

Fill in the Blanks

Alexander Van Dorn

Table of Contents

Chapter Two - Behavioral Tips and Techniques

Chapter Three - Bringing Your Templates Together

For the right to live as independently and productively as possible.

For the right to live, work, and play with the most freedom of choice.

PREFACE

Many professionals find themselves searching for assistance when creating individual Positive Behavior Support Plans. The internet offers very few templates but a considerable amount of assistance starting from scratch. The "gold mine" of templates shared in this book by author, Alexander Van Dorn, provide a basic foundation for creating your own individual Positive Behavior Support Plans. *All of the work has been done for you*. Just *fill in the blanks*, use information from the other templates, or mix and match information to create your own plans. Many of the templates provided have similar interventions and methods but are appropriate for many different behavioral challenges. Some templates are entitled the same but relate to different situations and approached in other ways. There are many easy methods to substitute the templates provided if you are unable to find the particular plan you seek.

Behaviors are effective and extremely efficient methods of communication. A Positive Behavior Support Plan is designed to increase positive behaviors while reducing, or replacing, challenging or dangerous behaviors. Most importantly, Positive Behavior Support Plans must be *personalized and specific* to the needs of an individual based on a completed functional assessment. Functional assessment templates are not provided in this book.

The Positive Behavior Support Plan templates provided have been written for adults who reside in community homes and who work or attend day programs. The plans may be modified for a school or home setting and may be used for the young and old.

The following are basic tips for using the templates:

1. Find all templates that apply to your needs. Review and prepare to mix and match, if needed. Remove entries that do not apply.

2. Consider the need to *individualize* your plans specific to the needs of the individual being supported.

3. Fill in the blanks provided with name of individual.

4. Consider the gender of the individual. Personal pronouns are listed as he/she, him/her, and himself/herself. Remember to change to the appropriate gender.

5. Entries of "Staff" should be modified to Teacher, QIDP, Consultant, Coach, Parent, or Administrator, whoever will be carrying out the plan.

6. Some plans discuss using law enforcement and reporting to appropriate agencies. If this, or any other section is not applicable, simply remove that section from your plan and insert your own information for follow through.

7. The location where the support will occur should be changed from home, to school, or to day program.

Positive Behavior Support Plans are designed so everyone involved works in the same consistent manner. Initially, a plan is created from a functional assessment which addresses an individual's challenging behaviors. It includes a focus on strengths, likes and dislikes, interests, and the goal to be achieved. The antecedents, behaviors, and consequences relate to the challenging behavior that is of concern.

A Positive Behavior Support Plan uses ONLY positive interventions and techniques to replace a targeted challenging behavior. No restrictive or unpleasant techniques should ever be used.

CHAPTER ONE

POSITIVE BEHAVIOR
SUPPORT PLAN TEMPLATES

PHYSICAL AGGRESSION

<u>Definition of the Behavior</u>

Physical aggression is defined as pushing, kicking, or hitting others. Historically, _____ will display this behavior when extremely angry. _____ may target staff or peers. Physical aggression may escalate to serious injury to others. _____ becomes upset when there are delays in access to desired activities, delays in responses to requests, inability to obtain sugar items or soda, requests to engage in activities which are not his/her choice at the moment, teasing by peers, when bossy to others and when he/she does not get a desired response.

<u>Support Plan</u>

1. It is recommended _____'s protocol for aggressive behavior be a "non-directive" approach when communicating with him/her. When _____ is refused, or told what to do, he/she is more likely to engage in verbally aggressive behavior, repeating him/herself, which may lead to physical aggression. Staff who work with _____ should be low keyed. They should be willing to rephrase requests, find different ways of communicating a message to _____, or even leave and approach the situation later. Staff who work with _____

should avoid making excessive demands where _____ does not feel there is a choice. Instead, staff should attempt to elicit cooperation by asking _____ to choose from a list of choices.

2. In addition, every effort should be made to determine _____'s interests and activity preferences. _____ should be given every opportunity, within reason, to participate in activities he/she specified. Over time a list of preferred activities will be developed that can be used contingently, or non-contingently, as part of a behavior support plan.

3. When _____ is becoming frustrated or upset, staff should make every effort to see the situation from his/her point of view. _____ needs to hear that staff understands how he/she is feeling and where it may be coming from. For example: "_____, I can see that you are feeling frustrated with _____ right now". In conjunction with this active listening strategy, every effort should be made to elicit communication from _____ when he/she is starting to become angry. For example, "_____, tell me what is bothering you".

4. If _____ continues to be anxious and shows signs of becoming physically aggressive towards someone, staff will firmly prompt him/her to stop. Staff will be firm but never harsh or scolding. Staff should emphasize teamwork among themselves while thinking ahead, being observant, looking for nonverbal cues, and having a course of action in place. Staff should create nonverbal signs instructing each other regarding redirection of other, utilizing crisis intervention techniques when necessary, and or making phone calls to the authorities.

5. While prompting to stop, staff will attempt to direct _____ away from the person that he/she has been physically aggressive toward. If any potential objects of harm are visible, or accessible, staff will remove others immediately. If possible, staff will attempt to engage _____ in a different activity as part of redirection.

6. If _____ does not calm, staff will redirect others from the area. Staff will never turn their backs and always maintain adequate physical distance from _____. Staff should avoid any power struggle with _____ and provide non-reactive monitoring unless he/she is being harmful to others. Once _____ has been calm for at least five minutes, no episodes or attempted episodes of physical aggression, staff will sit and talk with _____ about the episode. Staff will remind _____ that it is alright to be angry or upset. Staff will also help _____ problem solve more appropriate ways to express that anger.

7. Staff will remind _____ that he/she can always talk to them when upset. Staff will encourage _____ to go someplace quiet, away from others, until feeling calmer and more comfortable. The goal for staff is to listen actively with concern, encouraging open expression of feelings, and gaining an understanding of the crisis. Staff will maintain a calm neutral attitude and avoid words, gestures, and facial expression that suggest disapproval.

8. _____ responds to reinforcements such as candy, praise, being alone, watching television, and favorite foods, humor, music and 1:1 conversation. When _____ demonstrates an attempt to learn new coping strategies, _____ should be praised no matter how small the progress.

9. Staff will attempt to involve _____ in various activities. Staff will offer _____ a choice between two activities. Staff will ask "_____, what would you like to do?"

10. If _____ does not respond after the first prompt, staff will wait at least 1 minute before making another prompt.

11. While prompting _____ to participate, staff will once again suggest that _____ may want to participate in the activity.

12. If _____ still does not respond after the second prompt, staff will walk away. Staff will not make more than two prompts within several minutes.

13. If _____ appears to be upset, staff will ask if he/she needs to talk about anything. Staff will ask if anything is needed.

14. Staff will encourage _____ to express his/her needs to let them know how they can help. Staff will remind _____ they want to help him/her feel better.

15. If _____ indicates that he/she is angry or upset about something that someone has said or done, staff will let _____ know that sometimes people do and say things that are not appropriate. Staff will remind _____ that there are many people who care about him/her.

PROPERTY DESTRUCTION

<u>Definition of Behavior</u>

Property destruction is defined as intentionally breaking or destroying objects and throwing objects at a person or property. These behaviors usually occur when _____ does not get his/her way, is seeking attention, or is responding to "voices". Property destruction is usually in relation to _____'s temper outbursts.

_____ is most likely to destroy or damage things when anger has escalated from temper outbursts. _____ becomes angry when frustrated by something, or when he/she does not get a response he/she likes. _____ has learned to express his/her anger or unhappiness over something that has recently occurred by throwing and breaking things.

<u>Support Plan</u>

1. Procedures that apply to _____'s property destruction are for staff to always be alert, intervene early, remain calm and confident, and cue others to go to a safe area.

2. In support, staff will attempt to involve _____ in cooperative activities with his/her peers. Staff will attempt to involve _____ in games, crafts, and social activities that require working together with others. Staff will periodically praise _____ for appropriate behavior. Staff will praise _____ when working cooperatively with peers and treating their property appropriately.

3. Staff will be aware when _____ appears to be angry or upset with someone. When aware of any facial expressions, or body language that indicates that _____ is upset, staff will attempt to direct him/her away from the person and situation that is causing the escalation. _____ may tell staff he/she is upset which is a cue for staff to talk immediately and ask what is bothering him/her. Staff will tell _____ they think he/she looks upset and they would like to give him/her a chance to get away from whatever is so upsetting. Staff will remind _____ this will make him/her feel better. Staff will verbally praise _____ for walking away from the situation that seems to have upsetting. If _____ does not want to walk away, staff will attempt to redirect towards an activity that he/she finds enjoyable. Staff will praise _____ for walking away.

Intervention Plan

1. When _____'s frustration level begins to escalate, the important goal is to diffuse a tantrum from leading to property destruction. This is to ensure safety and minimize the audience. Staff to stay calm but firm. Staff should use visual prompts and avoid getting into to tantrum demands. Minor tantrums can be waited out by staff, monitored in a non-reactive manner, or interrupted in the early stages by helping _____ to focus attention on something else.

2. If _____ escalates to the point of attempting to misuse property, staff will verbally prompt him/her to stop. Staff will also

attempt to direct _____ away from the property and towards another activity.

3. If _____ continues the outburst and destroys property, staff will wait until he/she has been calm for at least 15 minutes, before talking with him/her.

4. Staff will remind _____ they know he/she was upset. However, staff will also remind _____ that this behavior was not appropriate. Staff will let _____ know what to do when he/she is angry and upset. Staff will give verbal prompts, if needed, and reminders of things that can be done the next time he/she becomes upset.

5. Once _____ has been calm for 15 minutes, staff will ask, when appropriate, to clean up any damage that has been caused. Staff will offer assistance.

6. If _____ refuses to clean up, staff will only prompt twice. Staff will not prompt a third time.

REFUSING TO COMPLETE
PERSONAL HYGIENE

Definition of the Behavior

_____will refuse requests to do personal hygiene tasks, particularly when asked to shower or change clothing. _____ may act unaware that a directive, or request, has been given. _____ may be obviously aware a directive has been given, but does not attempt to comply. _____ may overtly refuse to comply. _____ may attempt to change the conditions by arguing or ignoring staff. _____ will sometimes say "no," and sometimes become angry when asked to do something. Refusing to complete personal hygiene is defined as _____ refusing to follow staff's second request within 5 minutes.

Support Plan

1. Consistently providing effective cues can impact the amount of compliance that follows. A cue must be presented so that it is clearly understood and the expected response must be a behavior that _____ is able to perform under the circumstances.

2. Effective cues are clear, concise, and meaningful. They are communicated in a manner which is readily understood and processed by _____. A cue is used to prompt a behavior which _____ is able to do. Cues must be presented without excess emotion, close to _____, and after obtaining attention.

Examples of effective cues:

Calmly saying, "Please take your shower" rather than excitingly saying, "Take your shower now" Walking over to _____ and pointing to a symbol for "cool off" rather than loudly saying across the room, "Go cool off!!"

3. Sometimes resistive behavior may be due to deliberate refusal or just lack of understanding. It is effective to provide cues in three steps. First use a verbal cue. Secondly, use a visual prompt such as a picture sign or gesture. Last, a physical prompt such as a gentle touch or physical assistance.

Intervention Plan

1. When providing _____ a directive or making a request, staff to use effective cueing procedures and immediately turn and walk away or turn attention to another task. Periodically return to _____ and cue again. Do not linger to hear _____'s complaints or arguments. Walking away helps to avoid being drawn into _____'s delay tactics. It is very easy to be drawn into arguments or _____'s delay tactics. Once this is realized, staff should stop responding immediately, turn and walk away.

2. Staff to reinforce _____ with verbal praise or a gentle touch for compliance. Repeat this as necessary. In the early stages of intervention, compliance seldom occurs. Reinforcement, praise, something _____ likes or needs, should be provided each time

compliant. As _____ begins to follow requests more frequently the reinforcement may be faded out to every 3-5 times compliance occurs. Over time the reinforcement can be faded out even more as _____ is compliant for the entire activity.

3. Advantages to _____'s increasing compliance will be decreased safety risks, less frustration by staff, increased frequency of positive interactions, and increased repertoire of learned skills.

4. Staff will continue to recognize the importance of being flexible, offering _____ frequent choices, and avoiding engaging in power struggles.

5. Staff will encourage _____ to be as independent, as possible. Staff will attempt to engage _____ to complete as many tasks as independently as possible. Staff should praise _____ for any efforts made to be more independent and not make excuses for someone else to do things for him/her. Staff should remind _____ he/she is capable of many things and what a good job he/she does independently.

EMOTIONAL OUTBURSTS
VERBAL AGGRESSION

<u>Definition of Behavior</u>

Emotional outbursts include verbal aggression, yelling, crying and arguing. _____'s emotional outbursts appear to be a way of avoiding or escaping a situation or demand that is found to be unpleasant or does not want to complete. This is one of the ways _____ attempts to maintain control over a situation. _____ has a history of fluctuating mood, being stubborn, anxious, demanding, and exhibiting attention seeking behaviors. _____ has a history of yelling and using profanity towards others when upset. _____ may make more out of situations than they really are. _____ will manipulate circumstances to gain attention. These outbursts typically last 5 to 15 minutes and may lead to physical aggression or property destruction.

*Count as an episode when separated by 10 minutes.

<u>Support Plan</u>

1. Staff will attempt to involve _____ in various activities. Whenever possible _____ will be offered a choice of activities. When talking about the weekend activities ahead staff

will talk with _____ and engage in brainstorming preferred activities.

2. Staff will verbally praise _____ at random times for exhibiting socially appropriate behaviors. Staff will tell _____ that they appreciate it when he/she acts responsibly. For example, "Thank you _____ for participating, I really appreciate your help," or "You are doing a great job _____!"

3. If _____ appears to be upset, staff will ask if everything is okay. Staff will remind _____ they are available to help.

4. Staff will make _____ aware of any designated time to come back to them to talk.

5. If _____ does not want to talk, staff will suggest doing basic deep breathing exercises, listen to calming music, or going to a place to calm down, for example the back yard. _____ may be given the option of going into a room to be alone if wishes.

6. Staff will have ongoing conversations with _____ about the situations and people that cause anxiety. Staff will discuss what causes _____ to be angry and frustrated. Staff will tell _____ they want to help figure out what gets him/her upset and learn more appropriate ways to deal with his/her anger and anxiety. Examples may include: talking to staff person, walking away from the person when upset, going into bedroom, and learning relaxation exercises with staff.

7. Staff will always be gentle, but firm when confronting _____ about something inappropriate that may have been done. Staff will remind _____ that everyone makes mistakes and they will always try to help with correcting any mistakes that have been made.

8. If _____ appears to be embarrassed or upset about something, staff will calmly talk to about the situation. Staff will

not be scolding or reprimanding in anyway. Staff should also ask
_____ if he/she would rather talk about this in another
room.

9. If _____ asks for something that may not be available at
that time, staff will always phrase things positively and explain
why the item may not be obtained at the moment. For example, if
_____ wants to go out to eat, staff will explain, "This is a
great idea and we will find a time to do this. But, today we are
scheduled to make dinner at home".

Intervention Plan

1. If _____ begins to become agitated, begins to yell, or
begins making angry statements, staff will immediately prompt
_____ to stop and ask what is wrong. Staff should always
use a calm and neutral tone.

2. If _____ continues to exhibit a temper outburst, staff
will prompt him/her to stop once more and explain they understand
he/she is upset. Staff will explain they cannot help when he/she is
yelling and making angry statements. Staff should remind
_____ to make the point without using foul language.

3. Staff should redirect _____ into another room or
redirect his/her peers into another room and away from the
situation. Staff to determine which is more practical to the
situation; considering the number involved, how well
_____ is responding, and how many staff are present.
Staff must remember that during a temper outburst _____
perceives others as making fun or being hard on him/her.4. Staff
should encourage _____ to use deep breathing exercises,
listen to music, watch television or engage in another activity in an
attempt to calm self. Staff will remind _____ that ignoring
others and calming down will help achieve his/her goals.

5. If _____ continues to have outburst, staff will walk away for a few minutes. Staff will tell _____ to come talk when calm and ready.

6. Once _____ has been calm for several minutes, staff will also remind _____ they want to help but cannot when upset. For example, staff saying, "_____ if you are upset or frustrated you can tell me what is wrong or bothering you. I cannot help or understand you when you are yelling."

7. Staff will explain to _____ they like to spend time with him/her and are happy to help but that they also have to spend time with his/her peers. Staff will, when possible, set times with _____ to spend 1:1 time and remind him/her when those times are.

8. Once _____ has been calm for 10 minutes, staff will try to talk about the incident. Staff will encourage _____ to talk when upset.

9. Staff will help _____ determine more appropriate things that can be done do the next time he/she becomes upset about something, such as breathing exercises or coming to staff first with concern.

10. Staff will never attempt to force _____ to apologize to the other person.

THEFT

<u>Definition of Behavior</u>

_____ has a history of taking items that belong to others.
This may be in the community, at work program, from peers, or
from the kitchen. Theft is usually focused on soda, products that
contain sugar, or personal items _____ may want.
_____ is very sneaky and will hide items in clothing.
Records indicate that _____ will take anything wanted at
the moment and thinks can be hidden. _____ states he/she
does not worry about the consequences of this behavior.
_____ continues to take things that do not belong to
him/her. It seems _____ has been able to manipulate or
convince others to give "another chance" just by saying, "I'm
sorry".

<u>Support Plan</u>

1. People steal for a number of reasons, many of which may be
very complicated to understand. Stealing may occur when people
are in a situation they unable to control, or when they feel there is
no other option. For example, _____ resides in a board

and care home and has access to very limited spending money. _____ may steal to get attention, to find excitement in stealing, like the thrill of the act or simply want an item he/she does not have.

2. When _____ steals there are usually triggers. _____ has a desire to consume sugar. When in a store there are large quantities of sugar easily available. _____ may not have the money to purchase the item, or knows it is medically not advised, so feels compelled to reach out and take the item. This will provide _____ with the sugar wanted, the thrill of the act, and the attention if caught.

3. Issues of trust need to be addressed with _____. The key to helping _____ when caught stealing will be to understand the reasons why _____ may steal. How do we understand _____? We listen to the answers provided to the question, "Why do you steal?" When we listen to _____'s stories. We will find out the cause that pushes _____ to steal in the first place. Once we find out why _____ steals, then we can begin the helping process. Still, _____ can only be helped if accepts the help and is ready for it. The best way to deal with the problem of stealing is to address the root causes, which in _____'s case may either be personal desire, attention-seeking, or the presence of his/her auditory and visual hallucinations.

Intervention Plan

1. Throughout the day, staff will remind _____ of things he/she enjoys. These rewards could be going shopping, going out for a hamburger, buying something he/she wants, and outings he/she is looking forward to going on.

2. Staff will be alert to _____'s early warning signs. _____ may be behaving in secretive ways, appearing distracted, or being focused elsewhere. When these signs are

recognized, staff should intervene with pre-planned strategies. Staff should observe and monitor _____'s behavior very closely, especially in the house when near the kitchen or a community store.

3. Examples of strategies would be to reinforce acceptable behaviors and redirect inappropriate behavior. Staff will decrease stimulation around _____. Staff will use problem solving strategies with _____ and talk about the reasons or consequences of stealing. If _____ is agitated, staff will talk about what is bothering him/her. Staff should help _____ to focus attention on positive thoughts and other things. Staff will discuss ways _____ may obtain an item in a legal and more acceptable manner.

4. If _____ is found to have stolen an item, staff will maintain a non-emotional tone of voice and non-threatening body language. Staff will assist _____ in returning the item. If _____ has opened the item, he/she should be escorted to the store manager, peer, staff, to hand it back and say he/she is sorry. Staff should not discuss the incident with _____ when it is over. _____ should not receive any more attention to the matter.

5. _____ may be embarrassed or angry if found stealing. This may lead to anxiety or agitation. Staff will attempt to involve _____ in an activity. _____ will be offered a choice between at least two activities. Staff will ask "_____, what would you like to do?"

6. If _____ does not respond after the first prompt, staff will wait at least 1 minute before making another prompt. If _____ still does not respond after the second prompt, staff will walk away. Staff will not make more than two prompts within several minutes.

7. When appearing upset, staff will ask _____ to talk. Staff will remind _____ they want to help him/her feel better.

When speaking with _____, staff will talk about the importance of trusting one another and positive relationships.

8. Staff will be gentle, but firm when confronting _____ about something inappropriate that has been done, such as stealing. Staff will remind _____ that everyone makes mistakes and they will always try to help correct any mistakes that have been made.

9. Staff will not scold or reprimand _____. Staff will always remember to intervene as early as possible to interrupt or diffuse the situation before it occurs. Staff will remain calm for clear thinking and help other staff to remain calm. Staff to minimize talking and use visual cues with _____. Staff to arrange the area to allow for increased personal space. If possible, remove _____ from the situation and minimize the audience. Once calm, redirect and refocus _____'s attention. Staff to be positive and supportive.

10. It is imperative that staff do not give in to _____ when saying, "Sorry" and "I will not steal again". For instance, if he/she has a shopping trip that has been planned this should not take place the day of the theft. Staff will tell _____ the shopping trip will occur another time and remind _____ if found stealing there will not be a reward going shopping. _____ should be reminded of the trip periodically throughout the day so he/she does not forget and is able to focus on earning it. Staff will talk with _____ about the consequences of stealing behavior when it occurs.

AWOL

<u>Definition of Behavior</u>

This is defined as going beyond the perimeter of the home without staff supervision or knowledge. _____ will leave the home and when in the community call 911 to have him/herself 5150'd.

Staff chart each episode of leaving the home without supervision or knowledge by others.

<u>Support Plan</u>

1. Staff will engage _____ in various activities at home and in the local community. They will offer _____ choices between activities whenever possible.

2. Staff will encourage _____ with praise for being independent and making appropriate decisions. Staff will remind_____ how much they enjoy being around him/her.
3. Staff will periodically check in with _____ and ask how he/she is feeling. Staff will remind _____ they are available

when needed or would like to talk about something. Staff will also ask if _____ would like to for a walk with them.

4. Staff will monitor _____'s moods to see how he/she is doing and what his/her emotional state appears to be.

5. Staff will periodically review and ensure _____ carries a current address and phone number with him/her. Staff will review this at least two-three times per week for consistency.

6. If _____ wants something that he/she is unable to have at the time asked, staff will always let him/her know when the item will be obtainable.

Intervention Plan

1. If _____ leaves the home without staff knowledge or supervision, staff will search the immediate area.

2. Staff will immediately contact the facility administrator if they are unable to locate _____.

3. Staff will contact supervising agency if they are not able to locate _____ within 30 minutes.

4. Once staff locates _____, they will check to make sure that he/she is not in need of medical attention.

5. Once staff determine _____ is medically stable, they will talk with him/her about the situation. Staff will explain they understand that he/she became upset/angry. Staff will also remind _____ that they are available to help him/her feel better.

6. Staff will remind _____ that it could be very dangerous for him/her to leave the home without staff. Staff will help _____ problem solve to remember safer things that can be

done the next time he/she becomes angry or upset about something.

THREATENING TO HURT SELF

Definition of Behavior

This is defined as making threats to injure him/herself in some way.

*Staff chart as a separate episode whenever there are 10 minutes between threats.

Support Plan

1. Staff will periodically engage _____ in various activities at home and local community. Staff will offer _____ choices between activities whenever possible.

2. Staff will encourage _____ with praise for being independent, making appropriate decisions, and reminding him/her how much they enjoy being around him/her.

3. Staff will periodically check in with _____ and ask him/her how he/she is feeling. They will also remind _____ they are available when he/she needs something or would like to

talk about something. Staff will also ask _____ if he/she would like to take a walk with them.

4. Staff will monitor _____'s emotional state.

5. If _____ wants something that he/she is not able to have when asked, staff will always explain when he/she will be able to have the item. Staff will remind _____ to verbalize and ask for what is wanted.

6. If _____ seems upset about something staff will ask if there is anything wrong and if there is something that can be done to help.

Intervention Plan

1. If _____ threatens, or attempts to hurt him/herself, staff will calmly remind him/her that they care deeply about him/her and do not want him/her to get hurt.

2. Staff will use appropriate Crisis Prevention Intervention Techniques if _____ continues to be dangerous to him/herself or someone else.

3. Once _____ has calmed down and has not attempted to hurt self for several minutes, staff will talk with him/her about the situation. Staff will also provide any necessary medical attention and support.

4. Staff will remind _____ he/she knows safer and healthier things to do when becoming upset. Staff will help _____ problem solve healthier ways to manage stress and frustration.

RESISTIVE TO REQUESTS

Definition of Behavior

_____ may act unaware that a directive or request has been given. _____ may be obviously aware a directive has been given, but does not attempt to comply. _____ may attempt to change the conditions by negotiating, bargaining, or arguing. _____ will sometimes say "no," and sometimes becomes angry asked to do something he/she does not choose to do.

_____ has been exhibiting avoidance behaviors where he/she is making excuses to avoid going to day program or completing daily skills and tasks. _____ has a history of becoming very stubborn and resistive when asked to do things he/she does not want to do. _____ commonly resists staff's requests to bathe, brush teeth, wash hands before eating and after bathroom use.

Support Plan

1. Staff will always offer _____ choices of activities and tasks. Staff will also try to be as flexible, as possible. An example

would be offering _____ a choice of activities or food items he/she likes for the completion of the activities of daily living.

2. When asking _____ to do something, staff will make their requests in calm yet firm tones. Staff will try to gain _____'s eye contact when they talk with him/her.

3. If possible, staff should always attempt to give _____ advance notice of appointments or activities of daily living that need to be completed. For example, "_____, you will need to shower in the morning, you have a doctor's appointment tomorrow afternoon." Staff will periodically explain to _____ the importance of completing hygiene tasks, attending appointments, and participating in house activities in regular conversations.

4. When providing _____ a directive or making a request, staff will use effective cueing procedures and immediately turn and walk away or turn attention to another task. Periodically staff will return to _____ and make request again. Staff will not linger to hear complaints or arguing. Walking away helps to avoid being drawn into _____'s delay tactics. It is very easy to be drawn into arguments or _____'s delay tactics. Once this is realized, staff should stop responding and immediately walk away.

Intervention Plan

1. If there is no response to a request within 5 minutes, staff will ask _____ once more stating they would appreciate his/her help or need him/her to complete a task.

2. Staff will explain why he/she cannot do something or the importance of his/her participation in an activity. Staff will always ask if _____ understands their reasoning and his/her thoughts/feelings are about it.

3. If _____ continues to ignore the request, staff will ask one of _____'s peers to complete a request. Staff will then praise that peer for following that request.

4. Staff will return about 10 minutes later and talk to _____ about the situation. Staff will explain _____ it is important to do things even if you do not want to do it sometimes.

5. Staff will positively reinforce _____ with verbal praise when compliant and responds appropriately. For example, "_____, thank you for helping me" or "I appreciate when you do this."

URINATES IN PLACES
OTHER THAN TOILET

Definition of Behavior

_____ is independent with bathroom tasks. During the day _____ will wet him/herself if angry or does not get own way. _____ will urinate during the night and wipe self with linens, clean clothing, laundry and towels. _____ will purposely urinate on the floor, in clothing or bed and refuse to use the toilet. This behavior evokes a strong emotional reaction from caretakers and is very effective in gaining attention. Every effort has been made since placement to discover the reasons for urinating in places other than the toilet. _____ will say he/she does not know, smirk at speaker, or say because he/she wants to. _____ also states it is because he/she "likes to" or feels lazy.

Support Plan

1. _____ responds well to 1:1 attention, immediate rewards, and positive reinforcement. _____ is very

33

motivated by family visits, shopping, and eating. Staff will periodically attempt to involve _____ to cooperative activities with staff and peers. Staff will attempt to involve _____ in games and crafts that require working together with others. Staff will periodically praise _____ for appropriate behavior. Staff will particularly praise _____ when working cooperatively with his/her peers and treating their property appropriately.

2. When _____ is upset, he/she may urinate on him/herself. Staff should remind _____ to use the toilet when aware he/she is angry about something. Staff to remind _____ they have many fun outings planned or something special on the calendar. Staff should let _____ know ahead of time what events will be occurring and utilize this as motivation to use the toilet when urinating. Staff will remind _____ of being an independent adult who should not need help with toileting.

Intervention Plan

1. Staff will attempt to diffuse situations and intercept before _____ chooses to urinate on the floor or in clothing. It is important that staff interrupt the behavior without any emotional reaction at all. Staff will redirect _____ to the bathroom. Staff will be aware of triggers and antecedents to reduce anxiety and stimulation levels which lead to more behaviors in the future. Staff will frequently encourage _____ to use the bathroom throughout the day and wipe self with toilet paper. This should also occur prior to going to sleep. Staff will praise _____ for urinating in the toilet and wiping self properly.

2. Staff will explain why _____ needs to urinate in the toilet and wipe self properly using toilet paper. Throughout the day, staff should remind _____ of things he/she enjoys or will earn for not urinating in inappropriate places and wiping self with toilet

paper. _____ enjoys going for a hamburger, buying things, or going outing. These can all be used for motivational purposes.

3. Staff will NEVER talk about the consequences of _____'s inappropriate urination when feeling angry or upset. This will only escalate the situation. Staff will also remember not to take _____'s behavior personally. It must be understood staff run the risk of escalating the situation if they take it personally or respond in a negative or hostile way towards _____.

4. Since _____ is urinating in inappropriate places and wiping self with things other than toilet paper, staff should be very aware of times _____ becomes quietly upset. This is an indicator of when this behavior may occur. _____ should be part of cleaning up and doing laundry tasks when this occurs. _____'s personal belongings should never be removed and _____ must understand he/she will earn outings, and special events when using the toilet.

5. When _____ urinates on the floor, or in clothing, staff will provide as little attention, interaction, or response as possible. _____ expects staff to become upset. Staff will ask _____ to clean up the mess. If _____ refuses after two requests, staff will begin to clean it themselves without any discussion or response. _____ should not be able to see any reaction at all.

6. Staff will ignore negative behaviors, reinforce, and respond to _____'s positive behaviors. _____ should be praised and rewarded for any efforts made, no matter how small. _____ will soon experience motivating rewards are a better way than negative urination on the floor and wiping self with things other than toilet paper.

WIPES SELF USING LINENS, CLOTHING, AND TOWELS

<u>Definition of Behavior</u>

_____ is independent with his/her bathroom tasks, but sometimes chooses not to use the bathroom. Instead, _____ will urinate and defecate in his/her clothing, bedding, or on the floor. _____ will wipe him/herself using the towels hanging in the bathroom, or uses his/her linens, clean or dirty laundry, and other cloth items to wipe him/herself. When _____ is angry or does not get his/her own way _____ may choose to purposely soil, or wet him/herself, then use something other than toilet paper to clean him/herself. Since this behavior evokes a strong emotional reaction from caretakers and is very effective for _____ to gain attention from staff even though it is negative.

<u>Support Plan</u>

1. _____ responds well to 1:1 attention, immediate rewards, and positive reinforcement. _____ is very

motivated by family visits, shopping, and eating. Staff will involve _____ to cooperative activities with staff and peers. Staff will involve _____ in games and crafts that require working together with others. Staff will periodically praise _____ for appropriate behavior.

2. Staff will be aware when _____ appears to be angry or upset with someone. When aware of any facial expressions or body language that indicates that _____ is upset, staff will direct him/her away from the person and situation that seems to be causing tension. Staff will tell _____ he/she looks upset and would like to give him/her a chance to get away from whatever is so upsetting. This is so _____ may not feel the need to urinate or defecate on him/herself.

3. When _____ is upset, he/she may urinate or defecate purposely. _____ often uses linens and clothing to wipe self to "get back at" or to attempt to provoke staff. Staff will remind _____ to use toilet paper to wipe him/herself. This reminder should occur when staff become aware _____ is angry about something. Staff should remind _____ ahead of time what events will be occurring for use as motivation. Staff will verbally praise _____ for directing him/herself away from the situation and after using the toilet using toilet paper which staff ensured is available.

Intervention Plan

1. Staff will attempt to diffuse situations and intercept _____ before choosing to urinate or defecate on self and then wipe self with things other than toilet paper. It is important that staff interrupt the behavior without any emotional reaction at all. Staff will redirect _____ to the bathroom to clean self thoroughly giving him/her appropriate items to use. Staff will be aware of triggers and antecedents to the behavior to reduce anxiety and stimulation levels that trigger this behavior in the future. Staff will encourage _____ to use the bathroom continuously

though out the day and wipe using toilet paper. This should also occur prior to _____ going to sleep. Staff will praise _____ for urinating/defecating in the toilet and wiping self properly.

2. Staff will NEVER talk about the consequences of _____'s inappropriate urinating behavior or wiping self with items other than toilet paper. When staff are feeling angry or upset this should be kept to themselves. This will only escalate the situation and give _____ pleasure for having evoked a negative response from staff. Staff will remember not to take _____'s behavior personally. Staff must understand they run the risk of escalating the situation, or reinforcing it, if they take it personally and respond in a negative or hostile way towards _____.

3. Since _____ is urinating in inappropriate places and wiping self with things other than toilet paper, staff should be very aware of times _____ becomes quietly upset. This is an indicator of when this behavior may occur. _____'s personal belongings should never be removed as a consequence.

4. When _____ wipes self with items other than toilet paper, staff will provide _____ with as little attention, interaction, or response, as possible. _____ expects staff to become upset. Staff will ask _____ to gather the soiled linens and then go to the bathroom and clean him/herself up. If _____ refuses after two requests, staff will begin to gather the soiled linen and walk quietly to the laundry room without speaking. There will be no further discussion or response. _____ should not be able to see any reaction at all. Staff to remind _____ of what he/she is trying to earn for positive behavior in regards to toileting and hygiene.

5. Staff will ignore negative behaviors. Staff will reinforce and respond to _____'s positive behaviors. _____ will be praised and rewarded for any effort _____ makes, no matter how small. _____ will soon experience motivating

rewards are a better way than wiping self with things other than toilet paper.

VERBAL THREATS OF AGGRESSION

<u>Definition of Behavior</u>

Verbal aggression is defined as yelling, threatening, and arguing. _____'s verbal outbursts are a way of avoiding/escaping a situation or demands perceived as unpleasant and does not want to complete. This is one of the ways _____ attempts to maintain control over a situation. _____ has a history of fluctuating mood, being stubborn, anxious, demanding, and exhibiting attention seeking behaviors. _____ has a history of yelling and using profanity towards others when upset. _____ is a long time smoker and much this behavior may revolve around the need to smoke. Other behaviors occur because _____ does not want to attend day program daily. These outbursts typically last 5 to 15 minutes and may lead to physical aggression or property destruction.

*Count as an episode when there are 10 minutes separating incidents.

Support Plan

1. Staff will attempt to involve _____ in various activities. Whenever possible staff will offer _____ a choice between activities. When making the activity calendar staff should talk with _____ and engage in brainstorming preferred activities. _____ responds well to 1:1 interaction, humor, and compliments.

2. Staff should verbally praise _____ at random times for exhibiting socially appropriate behaviors. Staff will tell _____they appreciate it when he/she acts responsibly. For example, "Thank you _____ for participating, I really appreciate your help," or "You're doing a great job _____."

3. If _____ appears to be upset, staff will ask him/her if everything is okay. Staff will remind _____ they are available to help and it may feel better to talk about what is bothering him/her.

4. Staff will also make _____ aware of any designated time when he/she can come back to and talk when staff are free and or ready to have a conversation.

5. If _____ does not want to talk, staff will suggest doing basic deep breathing exercises, listen to calming music, or go to a place to calm down, for example the back yard. _____ may also be given the choice to go into a room to be alone, if wishes.

6. Staff will have ongoing conversations with _____ about those situations and people that cause anxiety, anger, or frustration. Staff to help figure out what causes these feelings and teach more appropriate ways to deal with anger and anxiety. These might include: talking to staff, walking away from the person that is upsetting, going to bedroom, or learning to do relaxation exercises with staff when upset.

7. Staff should always be gentle, but firm when confronting _____ about something inappropriate that has been done. Staff will remind _____ that everyone makes mistakes and they will always try to help correct any mistakes made.

8. If _____ appears to be embarrassed or upset about something, staff will calmly talk about the situation. Staff will not be scolding or reprimanding in anyway. Staff will also ask _____ if he/she would rather talk about this in another room.

9. If _____ asks for something that may not be available at that time, staff will always phrase things positively and explain why it cannot occur at the moment. For example, if _____ wants to go out to eat, staff will explain this is a great idea and they will help find a time to do this. Staff to explain that today they are scheduled to make dinner at home.

Intervention Plan

1. If _____ appears to be agitated, begins to yell, or makes threatening statements staff will immediately prompt _____ to stop and ask what is wrong. Staff should always use a calm and neutral tone.

2. If _____ continues to exhibit verbal aggression, staff will prompt to stop once more and explain they understand why he/she is upset. Staff will explain they cannot help when yelling and making threatening statements. Staff also remind _____ the can be made without using foul language.

3. Staff should redirect _____ into another room or redirect his peers into another room and away from the situation. Staff to determine which is more practical to the situation; number of consumers, how well _____ is responding, and how many staff are present when _____ exhibits verbal aggression.

4. Staff should encourage _____ to use deep breathing exercises, listen to music, watch television or engage in a different activity in an attempt to calm self. They will remind _____ that ignoring others and calming down will help achieve his/her goals.

5. If _____ continues the outburst, staff will walk away for a few minutes. Staff will tell _____ he/she can come and talk when calm and ready.

6. Once calm for several minutes, staff will remind _____ they understand he/she was upset. Staff will also remind _____ they want to help but cannot when yelling and making threatening statements. For example, this could include staff saying, "_____ if you are upset or frustrated you should just tell me what is wrong. I cannot help or understand when you are yelling."

7. Staff will explain to _____ they like to spend time together and are happy to help and involve him/her in activities. Staff to explain they also have to spend time with peers. Staff will, when possible, set times with _____ to spend 1:1 time together and remind _____ of those times.

8. Staff will never attempt to force _____ to apologize to the other person but ask if there is anything that would like to be said.

9. In addition, _____ will benefit from learning to recognize signals of early distress, Staff to teach _____ to manage stress levels without removing self to another area while experiencing an emotional outburst.

Calming strategies that can be taught and practiced by _____ include:

Using deep breathing exercises
Using relaxation techniques
Using small objects to manipulate, such as a stress ball to squeeze

Closing eyes and counting backward from 10
Lacing fingers together and stretching arms and hands out in front
of body
Looking away or closing eyes momentarily
Using positive self-talk
Watching television and movies

LEAVING WITHOUT NOTIFICATION

Definition of the Behavior

This is defined as leaving the perimeter of the home without notification to staff or not returning home at an agreed time. _____ has a history of AWOL behavior. This may occur when _____ is already upset, does not want to listen to staff, or when in possession of money and wants to go to the store. _____ is most likely to exhibit this behavior when recently had a conflict with staff or a peer. _____ may engage in this behavior when perceiving someone has said something unpleasant to him/her. This may be _____'s way of expressing anger or unhappiness over something that has recently occurred, or that he/she perceives has occurred. This may also be _____'s way of attempting to escape from a situation that is upsetting or unhappy. Antecedent conditions to leaving the facility without staff supervision or knowledge may include when _____'s requests, or needs, are not being met. It may also be due to how he/she perceives the moment, possibly as being ignored by staff or peers.

Support Plan

1. Staff will monitor _____'s moods and randomly express praise when doing something appropriate. Staff will tell _____ what a great job is being done managing his/her own anger in an appropriate manner without leaving the facility.

2. If _____ seems upset, or states that he/she is upset about something, staff will ask if to talk about the situation. Staff to remind _____ they care.

3. If _____ does not want to talk, staff will ask, if he/she would like to go for a short walk around the block. Staff will say they will need to go along but can give _____ space while walking.

4. Staff will always listen carefully to help _____ feel important and better.

5. If _____ wants something that is unavailable to have at the time, staff will explain and give a reason why. Staff will ask _____ if he/she understands why they are unable to obtain the item right then.

6. Staff will ensure that _____ carries identification that includes a current address and phone number. Staff will periodically review this information with _____ to make sure that accurate information may be provided, if needed.

7. Staff will periodically remind _____ to call 911 if alone on the streets and fearful or lost.

8. At other times throughout the day, staff will encourage
_____ to talk to others when upset and ask for help from
people. Staff will teach how to safely walk around the
neighborhood streets should _____ leave the facility without
permission. Staff will encourage _____ to become involved
in decision making and make choices for self. Staff will observe
_____ for signs of escalating agitation.

Intervention Plan

1. If _____ leaves alone, staff will attempt to bring him/her
back home. Staff will remind _____ that it is not safe to go
out by self when upset.

2. Staff will offer to take a walk with _____ if needs to
leave the home.

3. If _____ leaves and staff does not know whereabouts,
staff will search the immediate area.

4. Once _____ returns to the facility, staff will talk about
the situation. Staff will talk with _____ about the reasons for
becoming upset. Staff will remind _____ that leaving alone and
angry is not appropriate. Staff will ask _____ to tell them
what should be done the next time he/she is upset. Staff will
remind _____ that it could be dangerous to leave the home by
alone when upset.

5. If _____ does not return, the facility administrator will
determine how long to look before contacting the police.

6. The facility administrator will determine when to contact funding agency and inform them that _____ is missing.

PHYSICAL AGGRESSION
ASSAULT

<u>Definition of Behavior</u>

Physical aggression is defined as hitting, pushing, or any form of physical assault toward others. This behavior has the potential of causing injury to others. _____'s anger lasts about half an hour and then seems to calm self. Due to unpredictable reactions to frustration _____ can be physically aggressive toward others.

<u>Support Plan</u>

1. Staff will attempt to involve _____ in various activities, particularly those enjoyed most. _____ enjoys 1:1 time, sports, and skateboarding.

2. If _____ does not respond to staff's first prompt, staff will wait at least 1 minute before making anther prompt.

3. While prompting to participate, staff will once again suggest that _____ may want to participate in the activity. Staff should encourage _____ to try new activities to broaden interests.

4. If _____ still does not respond after the second prompt, staff will walk away.
Staff will not make more than two prompts within several minutes.

5. If appears upset, staff will ask _____ if he/she needs to talk about anything. Staff will ask _____ if anything is needed.

6. Staff will encourage _____ to express his/her needs and let them know how they can help. Staff will remind _____ they want to help him/her to feel better.

7. If _____ indicates that he/she is angry or upset about something that someone has said or done, staff will explain sometimes people do and say things that are not appropriate. Staff will remind _____ there are many people who care about him/her.

8. Staff will encourage _____ to verbalize his/her feelings, or to walk away from situations that are upsetting. Staff will also continue to be flexible by offering _____ choices for when chores and grooming and hygiene can be completed.

9. Staff should verbally praise _____ at random times for exhibiting socially appropriate behavior. Staff will tell _____ they appreciate it when observing appropriate behavior.

10. Each day, staff will talk with _____ about those situations and people who are upsetting and provoke anger. Staff will tell _____ they want to help figure out what is upsetting and to teach how to learn more appropriate ways to deal with anger. These might include: talking with a staff person, walking away from the person that has upset him/her, going into bedroom or elsewhere to calm down or listen to music.

11. If _____ appears to be upset, staff should sit and talk about it. Staff should ask _____ to tell them what can be done to make him/her feel better. Staff should provide any needed prompts. Staff should remind _____ that when upset he/she can go into other room, practice relaxation, listen to music, watch videos, or do something else that can helps to relax.

Intervention Plan

1. If _____ is physically aggressive towards someone, staff will firmly prompt to stop. Staff will be firm but never harsh or scolding.

2. While prompting _____ to stop, staff will attempt to direct away from the person that _____ has been physically aggressive towards.

3. Staff will attempt to engage _____ in another activity as part of the redirection.

4. Staff will also remind _____ to show or tell them when upset or angry. Staff will remind _____ that it is not ok to hit, or hurt, someone.

5. If staff attempts to involve _____ in an activity, and he/she becomes physically aggressive, staff will stop the activity for at least three minutes until calm.

6. Staff will periodically verbally praise _____ when acting appropriately and not physically aggressive.

7. Once _____ has been calm for at least five minutes, staff will sit and talk about the episode. Staff will remind _____ that it is ok to be angry or upset but they will also help problem solve more appropriate ways to express that anger.

8. Staff will remind _____ to talk to them when upset. Staff will also encourage _____ to go someplace quiet, away from others, until feeling calmer and more comfortable.

9. _____ responds to reinforcements such as being alone watching favorite television shows, videos, favorite foods, soft drinks, listening to music, and 1:1 conversation.

FALSE ALLEGATIONS

<u>Definition of the Behavior</u>

Making false allegations is defined as _____ making statements that a staff or peer has done something they have not done. When frustrated, upset, or manipulating the environment, _____ may make comments about others that are not true.

<u>Support Plan</u>

1. _____ has learned that making statements that may be untrue about staff or peers can be a very effective way to gain attention and reactions from other people. Staff will remind _____ it is important to be as careful, and as accurate, as possible when making statements about others.

2. Staff will remind _____ people may have difficulty believing things said if he/she sometimes misinterprets them. Staff will give _____ frequent attention and praise when for

honesty and being careful with the things said to people. Staff will try to minimize the attention given to _____ when it appears that stories have been made up. Staff should be aware _____ becomes agitated and frustrated when things are not perceived as being fair, there are not enough choices being given, or a situation needs changing to suit personal needs. _____ has shown from past behavioral outbursts, he/she is triggered by the environment and people around if it is demanding or lacks routine.

Intervention Plan

1. Staff will periodically remind _____ it is important to respect other people's personal boundaries and to tell the truth. Staff will remind _____ other people are likely to become upset if he/she does not speak the truth.

2. Staff will remind _____ it is important to be careful and honest about the things he says and the allegations made about others. Staff will remind _____ that people will only be able to trust him/her if they know the truth is being told. Staff will also remind _____ that people can get in trouble and hurt when allegations are made that are not true.

3. Staff will periodically praise _____ for being appropriate and respectful in his/her interactions with others. Staff will praise for being kind and considerate. Staff will also remind _____ how he/she appreciates it when other people are kind and respectful to him/her.

4. Staff will support _____ when they observe he/she is becoming agitated by the environment. Remind _____ to go to another room or outside in the back yard to "get away from it all", or to calm self. Staff will offer _____ time to speak 1:1 about what may be upsetting.

ALCOHOL AND DRUGS

<u>Definition of Behavior</u>

_____ has history of using controlled substances, alcohol to excess, and marijuana.
This has resulted in being arrested. (If this is case, define individual history)

<u>Support Plan</u>

1. Issues of trust need to be addressed with _____. Staff will talk with _____ about telling them when he/she plans to leave, where he/she is going, and when he/she will return. _____ should be reminded of the consequences he/she may face should he/she be caught drinking or using drugs or finding him/herself in trouble with the law. The key to helping _____ is to help him/her to understand the reasons why there is a need to drink or use drugs. Is he/she lonely? Is he/she depressed? Does he/she miss his family? Is he/she tired from a long day at program (job)? Staff will listen to the answers provided

to these questions. When we listen to these stories, we will find out the cause of temptation in the first place. Once we find out why, then we can begin the helping process. Still, _____ can only be helped if he/she accepts the help and is ready for it. The best way to deal with the problem of drug and alcohol abuse is manage the environment to provide little temptation and address the root causes, which in _____'s case may either be personal desire, attention-seeking, or a simple need for acceptance.

2. Staff will continue to talk with _____ regarding the possible consequences of this behavior, such as, incidents with law enforcement, being unsafe with impaired judgment while in the community alone, and side effects of alcohol and drugs with medications. Staff will continue to make _____ aware of the consequences so informed decisions may be made regarding him/herself and the future.

Intervention Plan

1. Throughout the day, staff will remind _____ of things he/she enjoys or can earn if not drinking alcohol or using drugs. These rewards could be going for a hamburger, buying something wanted, or an outing he/she is looking forward to going on.

2. Staff should be alert to _____'s early warning signs. _____ may be behaving in secretive ways, appearing distracted, being focused elsewhere. When these signs are recognized, staff should intervene with pre-planned strategies. Staff should observe and monitor behavior very closely, especially when _____ is making plans to leave for the community. Whenever possible, staff should shadow _____ when leaving the property without notification and observe his/her whereabouts and behavior.

3. Examples of strategies to divert _____'s leaving to drink would be to reinforce acceptable behaviors and redirect inappropriate behavior. Staff should change the environment and

offer a choice of activities or task. Staff should use problem solving strategies and talk with _____ about the reasons or consequences of drinking or drug use. Staff will help _____ to focus attention on positive thoughts and other things.

4. Staff will talk with _____ about his/her history, arrest record, and consequences of being arrested again.

5. If _____ appears to be upset, staff will ask if he/she needs to talk about anything. Staff will ask if _____ needs something. Staff will encourage _____ to let them know how they can help him/her. Staff will remind _____ they want to help him/her to feel better.

6. Staff will be gentle, but firm when confronting _____ about something inappropriate that may have been done. Staff will remind _____ that everyone makes mistakes. Staff will not be scolding or reprimanding. Staff will be positive and supportive.

SELF INJURY
HITTING HEAD IN WALL

<u>Definition of Behavior</u>

Self-injurious behavior is defined as any behavior directed at one's self that has the potential to cause injury. This is primarily defined as hitting head on the wall causing bleeding. _____ is most likely to display this behavior when having difficulty communicating or verbalizing needs and wants. _____ becomes frustrated which leads to self-injury (hitting head in wall) when loses toy truck, parts from toy truck, a quarter, or does not get own way when unable to communicate needs clearly.
_____ is least likely to experience this behavior with consistency in daily routine and when receiving an immediate response. This helps _____ to remain calm and reduce inappropriate behaviors.

<u>Support Plan</u>

1. It is extremely important that _____ maintain his/her daily routine with a variety of activity to avoid feelings of

loneliness, agitation, or frustration. _____ responds well to 1:1 attention and immediate responses to his/her needs.

2. Staff will provide a consistent daily routine for _____ with the opportunity for many activities he/she enjoys. _____ is to be given the opportunity to choose his/her activities and maintain personal control within a structured consistent daily routine. _____ must feel safe, secure, and cared for by staff.

3. _____ is currently enjoying individual attention, outings, and friendship with roommate, throughout the day. _____ continues with his/her current day program which allows stability during the day.

4. _____ does not initiate friendships but once established will maintain and enjoy them when in a stable and familiar environment. Staff to remind _____ he/she is safe and encourage interaction with his roommates.

Intervention Plan

1. If _____ begins to hit head in the wall, staff will prompt to stop. Staff will remind _____ this behavior is inappropriate and he/she is hurting himself. While prompting to stop, staff will attempt to direct _____ away from others and toward an appropriate activity. Staff to calmly ask _____ how they can help and explain they do not want to see any injuries. Staff to initiate this interaction immediately.

2. If _____ does not comply, staff are to remove others from the area should _____'s behavior escalate to physical aggression toward them. Staff is to provide NON-REACTIVE MONITORING, only necessary eye, verbal, and physical contact, reminding _____ to calm and stop hitting his/her head in the wall. Staff is to keep _____ within viewing distance to prevent any injury to self. Staff will immediately direct everyone

else away from _____ to minimize the possibility someone will get injured or view inappropriate behaviors. Staff will always use a firm, but calm tone, when talking to _____. Staff to gently touch him/her while asking to stop hitting his/her head in the wall.

3. If _____ continues to attempt to be self-injurious, staff will continue to direct the other individuals away. Staff will use emergency intervention techniques only if it is clear that _____'s behavior is immediately dangerous.

4. Once _____ has stopped hitting his/her head in the wall, staff will redirect to a calm place and sit together. Without pressure, staff will ask _____ what made him/her upset.

5. Staff will remind _____ they understand that he/she becomes angry. Staff to acknowledge these feelings are ok but remind _____there are appropriate ways to express anger. Staff to let _____ know they are there to help and will respond as quickly as possible when they see him/her becoming upset.

6. Staff to sit and talk with _____ about other ways to express anger such as taking a walk with them, walking away from people who make him/her angry, listening to music, looking at television, taking deep breaths. Staff to provide _____, when possible, with the lost toy parts, truck, or coins. Staff is to stay with _____ until calm.

7. When _____ has calmed down, staff are to observe for physical injury (apply first aid/ notify administrator), redirect to an activity he/she enjoys (leisure, household chores, etc.) and reinforce _____ for appropriate behaviors and responding in a safe adult manner.

GOSSIP

Definition of Behavior

Gossip is defined as telling others all that goes on with staff and/or peers throughout the day. This includes personal, medical and confidential information. _____ usually repeats what has been overheard from a conversation he/she was not involved in, or repeats what has been told in the privacy of the house.

*Count as a separate episode whenever there are 10 minutes between episodes.

Support Plan

1. Staff will attempt to keep their personal or private conversations to a minimum. Whenever possible, staff will speak in a low voice or in a private room when discussing information that should not be heard by _____.

2. Staff will also discuss with _____ the importance of private information and issues of confidentiality. Staff should clearly give examples of what kind of information is appropriate and inappropriate to discuss with others.

3. If staff needs to discuss an issue with _____ but would like for _____ to not give this information out to other staff or peers they should clearly state, "_____, this information is private and should not be discussed with others because it would be inappropriate."

Intervention Plan

1. If _____ is caught gossiping to, or about, staff or peers, staff should immediately intervene, telling _____ to stop talking about others. For example, "Please stop. It is not very nice to discuss other people's business without their permission or their presence."

2. Staff should redirect his/her peers in order to speak alone about the incident with _____.

3. Whenever possible staff should explain to _____ why it is inappropriate to gossip and remind him/her they have discussed this issue before in private.

4. Staff should reinforce the issues of confidentiality and privacy and then ask if the issues are understood or more explanation is needed to clarify.

5. Staff should give _____ their attention, and converse if he/she wishes to talk about another issue appropriately.

REFUSING MEDICATION

<u>Definition of Behavior</u>

Refusing to take medication is defined as _____'s refusing to follow staff requests to take his/her medication as prescribed. When asked to take medications _____ may refuse the first time. At times, _____ will eventually comply after staff offer additional time to respond. At other times, _____may become verbally or physically aggressive towards others after being non-compliant. _____ will sometimes scream and use inappropriate language. _____ is least likely to exhibit this behavior when staff are flexible and offer choices of when he/she may complete their request.

<u>Support Plan</u>

1. Staff will attempt to be flexible and try to offer choices of when _____ can complete the task within medication administration and prescription guidelines.

2. Staff should give _____ as much control and self-empowerment as possible. It is important that _____ have the opportunity to make choices and decisions about his/her own life and own schedule. Staff should talk with _____ about the importance of taking medication at the prescribed times so there is a better understanding and _____ is able to make informed choices.

3. When asking _____ to take the medications, staff should ask once. Staff should also ask _____ to repeat the request so that they are sure that it is understood. Staff should also try to obtain eye contact and speak loudly with _____ before making the request. This is in order to maximize understanding.

4. Staff will verbally praise _____ for compliance with the request. Staff will let _____ know they appreciate how helpful he/she is being. Staff will also thank _____ for being so mature and responsible.

5. If _____ does not respond after the first request, staff should wait at least one minute before asking again.

6. When making a second prompt, staff should ask _____ why it is important to follow the request. If the response is "I don't know", or "I don't care", staff should try to explain again. For instance, staff may remind _____ that the medications are needed to make him/her feel better.

Intervention Plan

1. If _____ does not want to follow the task, or does not respond, staff will ask when he/she thinks he/she would like to complete the request. If _____ is being practical and reasonable within the prescribed medication window, staff should support that request and allow him/her to wait a few minutes.

2. Staff should also remind _____ sometimes people need to do something that they do not want to do. Staff should generally not prompt _____ more than twice. After making a second prompt, staff should generally walk away from _____ for at least five minutes. Staff needs to remember that it may not always be important for _____ to follow each request immediately when it is made.

3. If _____ appears to be angry or upset, staff should attempt to talk about this. They should ask if anything is wrong. They should also ask if there is anything they can do to help _____ feel better. If _____ does not respond or states that he/she does not wish to talk, staff should suggest that he/she may feel better with some quiet time alone.

4. If _____ begins to use obscene language, or speak inappropriately, staff will remind him/her this is not appropriate. Staff will ask _____ when he/she would like to return to take medications explaining the importance of taking prescribed medications.

5. Staff to invite _____ to return again to take medications with awareness of the hour window prior, and after, prescribed time. If _____ refuses to take medications after all failed attempts, staff to document refusal and notify medical personnel.

6. Staff to continue to educate _____ regarding prescribed medications and the reasons for taking them.

SEXUAL ADVANCES
TOWARD OTHERS

Definition of the Behavior

Sexual advances toward others is primarily defined as any behavior that _____ directs towards others in a sexual manner, such as, standing too close and rubbing his/her body against others, putting his/her hands between his/her legs and rubbing private parts in front of others, and "humping" his/her body against others, or hugging too tightly. _____ will get very close to others. This appears to be a way of getting close to others to gain attention.

Support Plan

1. Staff will teach _____ everyone requires their own personal space. Staff will tell _____ not too touch or stand too close.

2. Staff will always offer a private alternative place where_____

can go if feeling sexual. Staff will also teach _____ the difference between private and public areas.   This may require staff showing _____ to the other room where it is private.

3. Staff will remind _____ it is not okay to try to get attention by attempting to rub his/her body parts on or near others persons.

4. Staff will take careful precautions to ensure that all other individuals visiting or residing in the home are redirected when this situation occurs.

5. Staff will always monitor _____'s interactions with his/her peers in an attempt to prevent any unwanted sexual advances.

6. Staff will periodically praise _____ for appropriate behavior. Staff will tell _____ how proud they are for acting appropriately and going to a private area.

Intervention Plan

1. Staff will involve _____ in cooperative activities and doing things he/she enjoys offering various choices. Staff will involve _____ in games and crafts that require working together with peers, such as building blocks, or drawing.

2. Staff will periodically praise _____ for appropriate behavior. They will particularly praise him/her when working cooperatively with peers and treating their property appropriately.

3. If _____ begins to make sexual advances toward others, staff will calmly let him/her know that it is inappropriate at that time and to go to a private area.

4. If _____ chooses to stop, staff will continue to monitor to ensure that he/she is not being intrusive toward others. Staff will talk to _____ about the incident remind him/her that needs will not be met by making sexual advances toward others. Staff will remind

_____of other things that can be done more appropriately to gain attention from others.

FOOD STEALING

<u>Definition of Behavior</u>

Food stealing is defined as _____ taking food from others without indicating in some way that he/she would like to have the item. This behavior includes food taken from peers and staff but also from complete strangers when he/she is out in the community. Most often _____ will focus intently on other people's soda and/or coffee. _____ will attempt to steal items such as soda or coffee whenever possible in public places.

*Count as a separate episode whenever there are 10 minutes between episodes.

<u>Support Plan</u>

1. Staff will attempt to feed _____ when they are also feeding his/her peers. Whenever possible, staff will offer _____ a choice between food items.

2. Staff will monitor _____ very closely when out in the community and attempt to steer him/her away from places where strangers with either soda or coffee are within close proximity.

3. When in a restaurant or near individuals who have coffee or soda, staff will remind _____ of his/her own personal drink and redirect when _____ begins to focus on another person's drink.

4. Staff will praise _____ by clapping and smiling. This will help remind _____ staff is proud whenever he/she eats his/her own food and does not attempt to steal it from others. Staff should also attempt to verbally reinforce _____ when he/she is behaving appropriately. For example, "Thank you for asking _____" or "Good job eating your dinner _____."

5. If _____ indicates that he/she does not want a particular food/drink item, staff will attempt to let him/her choose another item that does not belong to someone else, while explaining why he/she cannot have the item in question.

6. To further deter food stealing behavior, staff should write _____'s name on the drink and show that the drink is his/hers. This should occur out in the community whenever possible by bringing along name tag stickers with _____'s name written on them to stick onto his/her drink purchased in the community.

7. Staff should also engage in exercises with _____ to identify which beverages he/she can have. For example, place two cups in front of _____, one with his/her name written on it and one without and ask which drink is his/hers. If _____ gets the question right staff will clap and give the drink saying, "That's right, this one is for _____," while pointing to his/her name on the cup. In the event _____ points at the incorrect cup staff will say, "No, this drink is _____'s because this one has your name on it," while pointing to his/her

name on the correct cup. Staff should attempt to practice this exercise three times a day, or whenever _____ indicates he/she wants something to drink, allowing him/her to have the drink with the name on it.

Intervention Plan

1. If _____ begins to steal food/drink from others, staff will firmly prompt to stop, stating something like "that item is not yours _____. You cannot take it."

2. While prompting _____ to stop, staff will physically direct him/her away from others food/drink and softly put his/her hands in his/her lap reminding why he/she cannot have the particular item.

3. If _____ continues to attempt to steal the item staff will attempt to remove _____ from the situation and place him/her in an area where the behavior is less likely to occur. For example: at a separate table or in another room where the items are not present.

4. Staff should explain to _____ that it is wrong to take food or drinks from others without asking when they do not belong to him/her. Staff should go on to explain the importance of asking permission first before taking items from others.

VERBAL AGGRESSION
AUTISM

Definition of the Behavior

Verbal aggression is defined as _____ yelling at others in a threatening manner or communicating in a manner of significant disruption to others. _____ will make loud noises or sounds and walk at a fast pace. _____ will repeat his/her action over and over.

_____ has expressive speech and can communicate with others. Receptively, he/she seems to understand most things said to him/her. _____ appears to mutter things under the breath. _____ will carry on conversations with him/herself. _____ has some echolalic speech.

Support Plan

1. Staff should give _____ two to three options as he/she has difficulty transitioning from one activity to another. _____ needs to manage and navigate through the environment at his/her own pace. Feeling that there are options will give him/her a chance

to prepare and move through time and space at his/her own rate which may be different from others around him/her at the time.

2. Staff should praise appropriate behaviors liberally and as often as possible. Using positive reinforcement will encourage _____ to work toward his/her goals.

3. Staff should reward _____ for small things first and then lead up to more complex steps. Ask _____ how he/she would like to do it to get things done better.

4. Wherever possible eliminate sensory issues. If sensory issues are overwhelming, _____ may become verbally aggressive. Staff to observe to learn what over stimulates _____ in the environment. It may be loud noises, bright lights, many people, confusing demands, or irritating touches.

5. Staff to communicate with _____ verbally and ask what he/she is feeling, what he/she is doing, or if he/she is experiencing any possible pain, such as a headache.

6. Staff should remain as calm as possible when interacting with _____. Too many demands may push him/her over the edge and trigger self-protective or verbally aggressive behaviors.

7. Staff will be aware that _____ is very literal and a concrete thinker. _____ appears to be unable to "read" others body language and may not understand how staff is using language. It is difficult for _____ to understand another perspective.

Intervention Plan

1. Staff to encourage _____ to make choices in the activities he/she would like to pursue. _____ enjoys playing games, and memorizing. _____ should be encouraged to participate in activities that include social skills, such as, group "play",

activities that increase sensory issues, which could include activities of touch and handling, such as cooking, household chores, even petting a cat. To increase and expand speech skills 1:1 conversations should occur, as well as, listening to others express themselves.

2. Staff must be patient with _____ and let him/her know he/she is accepted, valued, and loved. _____ has many unique skills, talents, and abilities which he/she will develop with staff's praise and encouragement. Staff should present many opportunities for this development in giving choices in activities.

3. _____ should be given opportunities to socialize with others. This should begin in a safe and supervised environment. This will improve _____'s self-esteem and bring about opportunity to increase his/her social interactions in a positive way. Do not force _____ into social situations he/she is not ready for but teach manners, appropriate greetings, and how to politely make requests. Take gradual steps and do not request too many things at once as it may become overwhelming.

4. If _____ becomes verbally aggressive, staff will prompt to stop. Staff will remind _____ that his/her behavior is inappropriate. While prompting to stop, staff will attempt to direct _____ away from others and towards an appropriate activity.

5. If _____ does not comply, staff to remove others from the area. Provide NON-REACTIVE MONITORING (only necessary eye, verbal, and physical contact) until _____ is calm. Staff to keep within viewing distance to prevent any injury to him/herself or others. Staff will immediately direct everyone else away from the _____ to minimize the possibility someone will get injured. Staff will always use a firm, but calm tone and expression, when talking to _____.

6. If _____ continues to attempt to be verbally aggressive towards and possibly escalating toward physical aggression, staff will continue to direct the other individuals away. Staff will use

74

emergency intervention techniques only if it is clear that
_____'s behavior is immediately dangerous to other peers

7. Once _____ has stopped being physically aggressive, staff
will redirect _____ to a calm place and sit with him/her.

8. Staff to stay with (or nearby) _____ until he/she is calm
reassuring verbally that things are alright.

9. Staff will remember not to take _____'s behavior
personally. They will understand they run the risk of escalating the
situation if they take it personally or respond in a negative or
hostile way towards _____.

10. When _____ has calmed down, staff to redirect him/her
to an activity he/she enjoys, such as playing games, and verbally
praise for appropriate interaction/behaviors and responding in an
adult manner.

*Check recipient of aggression for injuries and give lots of positive
attention.

EMOTIONAL OUTBURSTS
AUTISM

Definition of the Behavior

Emotional outbursts are defined as engaging in screaming, hitting, scratching, throwing self to floor, overturning furniture, deliberate injury to him/herself, other disruptive behaviors associated with frustration or sensory "overload". _____ is easily frustrated when playing games and does not like to lose. He/she experiences sensory overload when exposed to too much noise or stimulation. He/she will clap or rub his hands together and will say "sorry" over and over. He/she will hit self in the face during tantrums. _____ also has a history of running into the street and throwing things at moving vehicles.

Support Plan

1. Staff should give _____ two to three options as he/she has difficulty transitioning from one activity to another. _____

needs to manage and navigate through the environment at his/her own pace. Feeling that _____ has options will give a chance to prepare and move through time and space at his/her own rate which may be different from others around him/her at the time.

2. Staff should praise appropriate behaviors liberally and as often as possible. Using positive reinforcement will encourage _____ to work toward his/her goals.

3. Staff should reward _____ for small things first and then lead up to more complex steps. Ask _____ how he/she would like to do it to get things done better.

4. Wherever possible eliminate sensory issues. If sensory issues are overwhelming _____, he/she may become verbally aggressive. Staff to observe to learn what over stimulates _____ in the environment. It may be loud noises, bright lights, many people, confusing demands, or irritating touches.

5. Staff to communicate with _____ verbally and ask him/her to articulate what he/she is feeling, what he/she is doing, or even if he/she is experiencing any possible pain, such as a headache.

6. Staff should remain as calm as possible when interacting with _____. Too many demands may push him/her over the edge and trigger self-protective or verbally aggressive behaviors.

7. Staff to be aware that _____ is very literal and a concrete thinker. _____ appears to be unable to "read" others body language and may not understand how staff is using language. It is difficult for _____ to understand another's perspective.

Intervention Plan

1. Staff to encourage _____ to make choices in the activities he/she would like to pursue. _____ enjoys playing games,

and memorizing. _____ should be encouraged to participate in activities that include social skills, such as, group "play", activities that increase sensory issues, which could include activities of touch and handling, such as cooking, household chores, even petting a cat. To increase and expand speech skills, 1:1 conversations should occur. Encourage listening to others.

2. Staff must be patient with _____ and let him/her know he/she is accepted, valued, and loved. _____ has many unique skills, talents, and abilities which he/she will develop with staff's praise and encouragement. Staff should present _____ with opportunities for this development in giving choices in activities.

3. _____ should be given opportunities to socialize with others. This should begin in a safe and supervised environment. This will improve _____'s self-esteem and bring about opportunity to increase social interactions in a positive way. Do not force _____ into social situations he/she is not ready for but teach manners, appropriate greetings, and how to politely make requests. Take gradual steps and do not request too many things at once as it may become overwhelming.

4. If _____ begins to have a tantrum outburst, staff will prompt him/her in a neutral but firm tone to stop. While prompting to stop, staff will attempt to direct _____ away from others and towards an appropriate activity.

5. If _____ does not comply, staff are to remove others from the area. Provide NON-REACTIVE MONITORING (only necessary eye, verbal, and physical contact) until _____ is calm. Staff are to keep _____ within viewing distance to prevent any injury to him/herself or others. Staff will immediately direct everyone else away from the _____ to minimize the possibility someone will get injured. Staff will always use a firm, but calm tone and expression, when talking to _____.

6. If _____ continues to tantrum this may lead to property destruction and possibly escalating toward physical aggression,

staff will continue to direct the other individuals away. Staff will use emergency intervention techniques only if it is clear that _____'s behavior is immediately dangerous to other persons.
7. Staff will always remain 3 feet or a handshake distance away when _____ is exhibiting antecedent or changing behaviors. Staff will remain neutral with their body language. Verbal cues must be presented in a neutral but firm method. A supportive stance in which staff feet are positioned in an "L" stance is recommended. Staff will never turn their back to _____ if he/she is exhibiting antecedent or changing behaviors.

8. Once _____ has stopped being physically aggressive, staff will redirect _____ to a calm place and provide 1:1 time.

9. Staff to stay with, or nearby, _____ until he/she is calm reassuring verbally that things are alright.

10. Staff will remember not to take _____'s behavior personally. Staff will understand they run the risk of escalating the situation if they take it personally or respond in a negative or hostile way towards _____.

11. When calmed down, staff to redirect _____ to an activity he/she enjoys (playing games) and reinforce with praise for appropriate interaction/behaviors and responding in an adult manner.

*Check recipient of aggression for injuries and give lots of positive attention.

FABRICATING STORIES ABOUT OTHERS

Description of Behavior

Fabricating stories is defined as attempting to manipulate a situation or a person either by cleverly situating objects or by making up a story that is not true in an attempt to be near or interact with a particular person. This behavior may include gift giving or attempting to buy something for staff and then making up a story about why the staff should take it. This behavior also includes _____ throwing away lunch, either purchased or packed from home, and begging others for food. It may also be a way of having staff buy something different stating, "I forgot my money", or "Staff didn't give me a lunch."

*Staff will count as an incident every time a separate attempt at manipulation/making up a story is made. If _____ is repeating the same story the incident will still count as one, this is not considered a separate attempt.

Support Plan

1. Staff will attempt to periodically talk to _____ and ensure he/she is receiving enough attention and is in a positive emotional state. For example staff might say, "How are you feeling today _____ ?"

2. Any time staff is talking with _____ about something they will use a calm, firm tone that will not provoke _____ to act out. Staff will encourage _____ to focus on activities and to keep conversations appropriate and honest.

3. Staff will promote honesty on a regular basis with _____ by explaining the importance of being honest and how it directly links to being trustworthy. Staff will reward _____ for honesty and appropriate behavior with their attention and positive verbal praise. Staff might say something like, "_____ I really appreciate all of your hard work today."

4. When staff check in with _____ asking how he/she is feeling they will give him/her an opportunity to talk with them 1:1. Staff should always make _____ aware of the amount of time they have, as to not be provoked by staff's inability to spend large amounts of time 1:1.

5. If _____ appears to be fixating on something, staff will ask what is bothering him/her. If does not want to talk about it, staff will let _____ know that he/she is able come when ready to talk. Staff will tell _____ they can better help when _____ is open with them about his/her feelings. Staff will let _____ know this is the time to plan/talk/ask about any issues because there may not be time available to do so later.

6. Staff will also practice basic relaxation training with _____ that consists of shutting eyes, counting to 10, and thinking about a special place, and slowly opening and closing the fingers on his/her hands. Staff will practice this training at least once each week. Staff will remind _____ the best way to

stop fixating on others is to take deep breathes and engage in an activity to keep the mind off of what is so bothersome.

7. If _____ makes a claim that staff is not sure is true, staff will ask _____ if he/she is sure about what is being said. Staff will let _____ know they are not sure if the story is accurate and they are giving a chance to change it. Staff will remind _____ he/she does not have to be afraid to tell the truth.

8. Staff will remind _____ that if he/she wants to be in a specific group or complete a specific activity these things have to be planned in advance when making the weekly schedule. Staff will explain it is just like working at a job. _____ may not get to choose whose group he/she is in or which staff member he/she works with. Staff will remind _____ to try and use the opportunity to work cooperatively with different individuals and make personal progress in this area. Staff may want to discuss with personal and behavioral goals at this time.

9. Occasionally staff will go over the program rules with _____ and ask to repeat the rules back. Staff will also include topics of why purchasing gifts for staff is inappropriate, how day program is not a place to attempt to get close to others, or try to find a girl/boyfriend. Staff will remind _____ of professional boundaries and encourage _____ to repeat these topics of discussion as well.

Intervention Plan

1. If _____ begins to make up stories or manipulate a situation, staff will tell _____ it is appreciated when being honest but they feel as if he/she is currently being dishonest. If needed, staff will explain why they feel this way. For example staff may say, "_____ I think you are being dishonest right now because I saw what happened. This is your opportunity to tell me the truth."

2. If _____'s statements involve stories about a staff member they will remind _____ not to talk about staff or his/her own personal life. Staff will remind _____ that day program is practice for work and personal issues or favorite staff preferences should not be discussed while working.

3. If _____ continues to manipulate a situation to try and be close to a staff, the immediate staff will ask the staff to take their group into another area. This is so the situation does not reinforce the idea that manipulation works to get close to a staff.

4. If _____ continues to insist that staff eat/drink/take an item deemed as a gift, staff will remind him/her why this is not appropriate and suggest the item be taken home instead. After reminders of boundaries there should be no additional attention paid.

5. When/if _____ stops manipulating a situation or telling a false story, staff should immediately reinforce the change in behavior by providing immediate attention. Staff will either start a new conversation with _____ 1:1 or engage in a preferred activity with him/her. Later on, if _____ is focused and in a positive emotional state, staff can specifically praise the change in behavior. For example; "_____ you did very well earlier today by turning your behavior around and stopping yourself from insisting that staff drink your soda. You should be proud of the progress you're making!"

6. If _____ persists with the manipulation efforts/making up stories about lunch items, staff will continue paying no additional attention to him/her. Staff will explain they cannot listen to stories that are inaccurate or while disobeying rules by trying to give gifts to staff. Staff will return several minutes later and begin talking with _____ again providing an opportunity to move on from the previous behavior. Staff will also tell _____ they appreciate it when he/she is appropriate and honest. Staff will remind _____ that it makes it easier for them to believe him/her when being accurate with what is said.

7. Staff will never accuse _____ of lying. Staff will always attempt to verify any statement that _____ makes or story told, even if that means verifying with others. Staff should remind _____ to be careful with what he/she says. Staff will also remind _____ to tell the truth if he/she wants other people to believe and trust him/her.

INAPPROPRIATE SOCIAL BEHAVIOR

Definition of the Behavior

This is defined as _____ approaching male/female staff and asking for personal information. This also includes _____ becoming angry, possessive, and jealous of male/female staff and their interaction with others. _____ has been known to follow around male/female staff too closely, talk or position self very close to this staff. This behavior is most likely to occur with new males/females _____ becomes infatuated with, most often a staff member.

Staff will count as a separate incident whenever there are 10 minutes of calm between episodes of asking for personal information, following too closely, becoming possessive or jealous of a staff's interaction with others.

<u>Support Plan</u>

1. Staff will regularly engage _____ in scheduled activities. Whenever possible staff will offer _____ a choice between activities. For example; "Would you like to play Checkers or Uno today _____?"

2. Staff will be as flexible as possible with _____ whenever planning activities but will keep _____ on task and engaged by prompting him/her to do the activity with them.

3. Staff will provide a physical activity for _____ to engage in at least once a day for approximately 10-15 minutes to an hour. This might include, jumping jacks, walking, basketball, or going to the park.

4. _____ will be reminded by staff everyone has their own personal space which they require in order to feel comfortable. Staff will carry ongoing conversations focusing on this issue at least 3x per week. Staff will physically show _____ how much space is needed in order to feel comfortable talking and interacting with someone. Staff will do this by extending their arm outstretched and point from their shoulder to their fingertips stating something like, "_____ remember to allow others at least this much space when you are interacting with them. This will allow others to feel comfortable interacting while with us"

5. Staff should also discuss with _____ how others do not appreciate when sexually inappropriate comments are made to them. Staff will discuss ways in which _____ can appropriately get the attention of others. For example staff may say, "_____ to get their attention you should say, excuse me, or hello I am _____." Staff will remind _____ this is a good opportunity to work on the way others are approached.

6. Staff will express verbal praise when _____ allows an appropriate distance between him/herself and others during conversations or participating in activities. Staff will say, "Good

job _____. I appreciate that you allowed that person enough space to feel comfortable interacting with you."

7. Staff will not rudely deny _____ appropriate physical contact. When appropriate, and _____ is having positive appropriate interactions with others or fully participating appropriately, staff will use some physical contact as positive reinforcement. This may be high fives, a pat on the back, or handshakes. Staff will remind _____ that as adults this amount of contact is considered appropriate physical contact at work and should be sufficient. _____will be reminded by staff not to be take advantage of when others are trying to be appropriate and friendly.

Intervention Plan

1. If _____ begins to violate someone's personal space, staff will immediately ask him/her to back up and give the person some space. At this time staff may remind _____ to extend his/her arm outstretched to double check the space being allowed them.

2. _____ should be praised verbally for following the staff's prompt when allowing for personal space, backing up after being prompted, or when checking the amount of personal space between self and others.

3. If _____ continues to violate someone's personal space staff to prompt a second time, in a louder and more firm voice. Staff's voice to remain calm. Staff to ask _____ to back up and allow the person some more space. Staff will remind _____ of being too close and that this is the time to practice allowing others personal space.

4. If _____ continues to talk in someone's face, follow them closely, or lean over their shoulder, staff will gently but physically show _____ the amount of space needed between others by

standing next to him/her and extending their arm out. While prompting, staff to step back in order to provide this space.

5. If _____ still continues to violate someone's personal space staff will prompt the other person to disengage their interaction with _____ and then redirect _____ into an alternate activity.

6. If _____ continues to hold, touch or inappropriately violate someone's personal space and the behavior begins to escalate, staff should immediately seek the help of another staff and make the administrator aware of the severity of the behavior.

7. If _____ is fixated or becoming possessive or jealous of a male/female staff, an additional staff of the opposite sex should redirect _____ back into an activity. Staff will remind _____ all of the staff need to work with others attending day. Staff will encourage _____ to take some deep breathes and calm down.

8. Staff will remind _____ engaging in this behavior could potentially affect his/her placement at day program or any opportunities to be out in the community during program hours.

9. If _____'s behavior becomes out of control or overly severe in anyway, endangering the safety of the consumers and staff, the administrator, the case worker and call the police to help with the situation. Staff will report this behavior to licensing by method of Special Incident Report.

10. Staff will document what happened prior to the incident, a description of the behavior engaged and all attempts made to redirect _____ as well as the method necessary in order to stop the behavior in order to keep the other person safe.

INAPPROPRIATE SEXUAL BEHAVIOR

<u>Definition of the Behavior</u>

Inappropriate sexual behavior is defined as _____ touching others without their permission in an attempt to flirt or invite them to touch him/her. _____ will tickle staff and peers, rub their person, grab others to pull them near or even make sexual gestures/invitations toward them. This behavior takes place both within the program facility and in the community.

*Staff will count as a single incident each time a separate action of sexual behavior takes place.

<u>Support Plan</u>

1. Staff will regularly engage _____ in scheduled activities while at the facility. Whenever possible staff will offer _____ a choice between activities. For example; "Would you like to play cards today _____?"

2. Staff will be as flexible as possible with _____ whenever planning activities but will keep _____ on task and engaged by prompting to do the activity with them.

3. Staff will provide a physical activity for _____ to engage in at least once a day for approximately 10-15 minutes to an hour. This might include exercising on the bike or treadmill with staff supervision, or going to the park. This will help to reduce energy and sexual drive. If possible staff should engage in the physical activity with _____ or make it a group activity so as not to single _____out and to encourage participation in the physical activity.

4. Whenever _____ is behaving appropriately staff will positively reinforce _____ by saying things like "Good job!" or "Thank you _____" in a high pitch voice or approving tone.

5. From time to time when _____ completes a staff request or acts appropriately staff will give _____ appropriate physical contact such as a pat on the back, high fives, or a light touch on the arm. Staff should explain to _____ why these actions are appropriate physical touches. Staff will also remind _____ that other touches are not appropriate while at day program.

6. Staff will explain to _____ that is not acceptable to rub, touch or tickle others. Staff will remind _____ that as adults this kind of physical touch is not appropriate while at day program because this is practice for work. Staff will also explain that people have personal space preferences that need to be respected in order for others to feel comfortable and want to be around us more often.

7. Staff will also remind _____ they will respond to his/her wants and needs by observing when she wants something or is attempting to get someone's attention. Staff will remind _____ that if he/she wants attention, or to engage in conversation, to simply ask others who respond. Staff will remind

_____ there is no need for physical touch in order to obtain these things.

Intervention Plan

1. If _____ attempts to touch another individual in a sexually inappropriate way staff will immediately prompt to stop. Staff will use a low tone and strong voice. Staff may say, "_____, stop. You need to keep your hands to yourself." This might include attempts at rubbing, touching, tickling or even hugging/kissing others.

2. Staff will ask _____ to come and speak with them privately, (if not possible staff should lower their voice so that peers are unable to hear) and explain to _____ it is inappropriate touch others and hands need to be kept to self. Staff will use a serious voice and make eye contact with _____. If in a private conversation, staff will remind _____ not only is this inappropriate but that these actions could have serious consequences like arrest or jail time.

3. Staff should always redirect _____ into another activity after explaining the behavior is inappropriate. This activity should not include the person that _____ touched or attempted to touch.

4. If _____ does not stop touching another individual staff will softly but physically stop _____ from touching others by directing his/her hands away from the other person. When applicable, staff will prompt others to leave or go into another room to avoid continuous contact. If the targeted person is the staff person providing services, another staff should be signaled for assistance. The other staff person should begin the redirection and conversations of appropriate behavior.

5. If _____ continues to be sexually inappropriate and the behavior becomes dangerous to others, staff will carefully document each time the behavior was dangerous to someone.

Staff will indicate all of the following:

a. Date and time that the dangerous behavior occurred
b. A description of _____'s behavior that required serious intervention to stop   injury/harassment
c. A description of redirection attempted before injury occurred
d. Staff person who had to intervene to prevent injury
e. Staff person witnessing the intervention

6. Once _____ has been calm and not sexually aggressive, for 10 minutes, staff will try to talk about the incident. Staff will again remind _____ that it is not acceptable to touch others inappropriately especially without their consent and that doing so is wrong. Staff should remind _____ this could result in an arrest or jail time. Staff will remind _____ that it is important to respect other people's privacy and personal space in order for them to feel comfortable.

7. Staff will help _____ determine more appropriate things that can be done the next time he/she seeks physical contact or to be engaged in an activity. For example staff might determine that a hand shake or a high five is more appropriate. Staff will remind _____ touching others while at day program is inappropriate and that this violates others personal space and makes them feel uncomfortable. Staff will encourage _____ to respect when others say no and respect when others say they feel uncomfortable.

8. Staff will closely supervise _____'s interactions with others at all times. Whenever possible staff will manipulate the environment or rearrange seating positions to reduce the likelihood that _____ will touch others by seating away from male/female peers or individuals being targeted.

INVADING OTHER'S SPACE
WANDERING

Definition of the Behavior

Inappropriate social behavior is defined as _____ following peers and staff around too closely despite asking for space, invading personal space/talking in someone's face, and bossing peers/acting like a staff. _____ will also complain about peers and their behavior in front of them, tease them or demand they follow his/her directions.

*Staff will count as a single incident each time a separate statement is made or inappropriate social action takes place.

Support Plan

1. Staff will attempt to periodically talk with _____ to ensure

that enough attention is being received and is in a positive emotional state. For example, staff will ask _____, "How are you feeling today? Are you having a good day?"

2. Staff will give an opportunity to talk with them 1:1. Staff should always make _____ aware of the amount of time they have, so _____ is not provoked by the inability to spend large amounts of time 1:1. Staff will remind _____ they have listened and now is the time to participate in activities and behave appropriately so that staff can work with everyone equally.

3. _____ will be reminded that everyone has their own personal space that they require in order to feel comfortable. This will occur through staff explanation and role model training from time to time. Staff should physically show _____ how much space is needed in order to feel comfortable talking/interacting with someone. Staff will model this by outstretching their arm and showing the distance from their shoulder to their fingertips where _____ can stand.

4. Staff will ask _____ to practice this technique with them and encourage checking the space left someone before beginning conversations. Staff will remind _____ that by doing this people will feel respected and want to listen and be around him/her. Staff will verbally praise _____ when for allowing an appropriate distance between him/herself and another during conversations or participating in activities.

5. Staff will also remind _____ of the 'golden rule'; to treat others the way he/she wants to be treated. Staff will have ongoing conversations that encourage empathy by putting him/herself in the other person's shoes and think about how it would feel if someone was teasing or bossing him/her around. Staff will remind _____ this is why we should not treat others this way. Staff will praise _____ for engaging in these conversations.

Intervention Plan

1. If _____ begins to violate someone's personal space staff will immediately ask to back up and give the person being interacted with some space. Staff will remind _____ of the modeling technique used and ask _____ to outstretch the arm so that enough space can be measured between them.

2. _____ should be praised verbally for following the staff's prompt when allowing for personal space.

3. If _____ continues to violate someone's personal space staff should prompt a second time, in a louder but still calm voice to back up and allow some space. Staff will remind _____ to use the arm as a measure. Staff to remind _____ that allowing personal space shows respect for others as we want them to feel comfortable around us.

4. If _____ continues to talk in someone's face, follow them closely, be bossy, staff will gently but physically show _____ the amount of space needed between each other by extending their arm to measure against his/hers. Staff will model for _____ to stand several steps back in order to extend the arm. Staff will show her their shoulder to their fingertips and that _____ should at least allow this much space between self and others.

5. At this time, staff should also remind _____ to work on allowing people a comfortable amount of space and explain why it is important to do so. Staff will remind _____ that when people feel comfortable around us they will want to hang out and interact with us more often.

6. If _____ still continues to violate someone's personal space staff will redirect to another activity away from the person being targeted and discuss the issue of personal space with

_____ while engaged in that activity. Staff should also direct the other person out of the situation. If the person being targeted is staff, signal to another staff member to assist and redirect.

7. Once _____ has provided space staff should give praise and then engage _____ in redirection or conversation. Staff will repeat this method as often as necessary.

8. If _____ will not cease teasing, bossing or making demands of others, staff will separate him/her from. Staff should go over the program rules and have them repeated back so that _____ understands it is not appropriate to tease others, boss others, or make demands. Staff will remind _____ that this is a changing behavior being worked on for improvement and _____ needs to make good choices. Staff can then redirect _____ back into the group and praise for turning the behavior around if chooses to participate appropriately.

WANDERING/AWOL
DAY PROGRAM

Definition of the Behavior

Wandering is defined as anytime _____ gets up and leaves the programming area. _____ will wander around the programming area to look for male/female peers, to use the restroom without notifying the staff of the need to go, or to look for a more interesting activity. _____ also leaves the facility property line without notifying a staff person and leaving the group while in the community to do what he/she wants.

Count as one episode every time _____ gets up and walks away from the assigned group without notifying staff and does not return within five minutes of being prompted to come back to the assigned group.

Count as one incident every time _____ runs out of the building and leaves the facility property line without notifying a staff person.

Support Plan

1. Staff will monitor _____'s moods and randomly praise him/her for staying with the group. Staff will say something like, "_____, you're doing a great job playing cards with your peers today! I really appreciate when you stay with your group!"

2. Staff will periodically remind _____ of the program rules about staying with the group or and telling staff where he/she is going so that they may go, too. Staff will remind _____ this is especially true if looking to go outside.

3. From time to time staff will encourage _____ to go on a walk with them around the outside of the building for fresh air. Staff will remind _____ this is an appropriate activity because he/she is accompanied by a staff member and that the whole group is participating.

4. If _____ seems upset when arriving to program staff will give at least five minutes to calm down before attempting to involve in an activity. Staff will also provide at least two choices of activities.

5. If _____ does not want to participate in the activity, staff will ask if _____ would like to complete another activity at that time. This alternative activity should occur in the same room as the scheduled group activity.

6. If _____ wants something unable to have at the time, a walk outside, staff will let _____ know when it is possible to complete that activity. Staff will remind _____ that there is a daily schedule and he/she helped to create the schedule the previous week.
7. Staff will have ongoing conversations with _____ which include the program rules both within the program facility and rules for being out in the community. Before any community activity staff will remind _____ that staying with the group is one of the rules and that wandering from the group while in the

community is dangerous and could jeopardize community outings in the future.

Intervention Plan

1. If _____begins to wander around the programming area, staff will immediately remind him/her to stay with the group. If _____ wants to move around the programming area staff will verbally notified of what he/she wants to do.

2. Staff will offer to take a walk with _____ if needed to leave the facility and if it fits into the staff schedule. If it does not fit into the schedule staff will give _____ a time that this would be possible.

3. If leaves the facility and staff does not know where _____ is, they will search the immediate area.

4. Staff will contact the police if they are unable to locate _____ within 15 minutes. Staff will then contact the police and _____ 's house staff.

5. If _____ is simply leaving the assigned group to do something different or participate with another group, staff will remind _____he/she chose the activity when making the group schedule. Staff will explain to _____ that it is important that we follow through with our decisions and that the activity currently being requested can be added to next week's schedule.

6. Staff will redirect once again by asking _____ to come back to the group to help complete the activity or sit with staff as others complete their activity.

7. If _____ continues to refuse to stay with the group staff will discuss the program rules regarding staying with the group. Staff to remind _____ if he/she continues to refuse

placement at day program or community outings could be jeopardized. (This is especially true if the behavior continues to occur in the community.)

8. Staff will tell _____ they always appreciate when directions are followed and they understand sometimes we have to do things we do not want to do. Staff will tell _____ they will try to accommodate his/her wants for the next activity and that he/she is always welcome to brainstorm preferred activities when they are coming up with an activity schedule for the upcoming week.

PICA
INGESTING INEDIBLE OBJECTS

Definition of the Behavior

Pica is defined as placing inedible objects in the mouth and swallowing them. For _____, this behavior typically includes eating cigarette butts while out in the community, although this can also include items around the facility most often food off of the floor. This behavior has yet to cause _____ any serious injury where medical attention has been required.

*Count as one incident every time an attempt is made or every time a non-edible item is ingested.

Support Plan

1. Staff will periodically offer _____ a variety of edible fruits, vegetables, etc. when at home. Staff will tell _____ these foods are okay to eat and will cause illness.

2. Staff will closely monitor _____ at all times while in the program facility and out in the community, watching for and avoiding possible situations that may elicit this behavior.

3. Staff will keep dangerous liquids out of reach from _____ at all times.

4. Staff will remind _____ when outside that certain plants, leaves, etc. are not edible and could cause illness by physically showing which ones are not edible.

5. Staff will praise _____ when able to leave drinks alone or go outside without attempting to eat any plants or leaves.

6. Staff will attempt to practice flash cards with _____ weekly to help identify items that are edible and not edible. Staff will use these same flash cards at times of intervention in order for _____ to better communicate needs and desires.

Intervention Plan

1. When _____ attempts to ingest an inedible object, staff will prompt him/her to stop. Staff will request _____ spit out whatever is in his/her mouth.

2. If _____ does not spit out the item staff will attempt to gently pull the item from _____'s hands and mouth.

3. Staff should always attempt to immediately identify what _____ has ingested and evaluate how dangerous the item is. If dangerous, staff should call the paramedics immediately. If seemingly not very harmful, staff should monitor _____ closely for the following hour to see what effect the item may be having and if there are still possible dangers.

4. Staff will periodically remind _____ that eating objects found inside or outside can cause illness. Staff will offer _____ an edible food to be eaten instead. In order to better communicate this to _____ staff will use flash cards with symbols of food and non-edible items and say aloud, "Yes, eat."

when showing food items and saying, "No. don't eat." when showing non-edible items.

5. If _____ ingests a harmful liquid or dangerous object staff will immediately call 911 and the facility administrator taking all precautions necessary to prevent further harm to _____.

SELF INJURY
PICKING SKIN/BITING SELF

Definition of the Behavior

Self-injurious behavior is defined as _____ scratching, picking at skin or scabs and biting hands or fingers. Typically _____ does not cause serious injury when exhibiting this behavior although some scratches need minor first aid.   This behavior last about a minute or so at the most as staff monitor this behavior and redirect _____ fairly quickly.

*Count as a separate incident whenever there are separate actions made.

Support Plan

1. Staff will remind _____ that everyone gets mad and upset at different times. Staff to let _____ know that it is alright to have a quiet place to go when upset or frustrated. Staff to have ongoing conversations with _____ that include explaining everyone gets angry, upset, or sad and these emotions are common.

2. Staff will always offer an alternative place somewhere quiet to

calm down. Staff will also attempt to teach _____ basic relaxation training that consists of shutting the eyes and taking deep breaths. This may require staff to physically show _____ to the other room and taking deep breaths, too, in order to demonstrate. This should be practiced daily.

3. Staff will occasionally remind _____ that it is not okay to try to get attention by attempting to hurt him/herself. Staff will tell _____ that this may cause serious injury and it will not get any needs met.

4. Staff will take careful precautions to ensure that all potentially dangerous and sharp objects are locked up and out of _____'s reach.

Intervention Plan

1. If _____ attempts to injure self, staff will immediately prompt to stop. Staff will direct away from the situation by taking _____ to a quiet environment until calm.

2. If _____ is unable to be redirected staff will back up and give _____ space while still monitoring the behavior. Staff will say, "_____ I am backing away from you to give you some time to calm down. I will come back and check on you in a few minutes." Staff will then pay no additional to _____. Staff will monitor from a safe distance.

3. If _____ hurts him/herself and is calm, staff will apply any needed medical treatment. Staff will document the incident and any intervention or treatment that was required.

4. If appropriate, staff will complete the required Special Incident Report and forward it to all relevant individuals.

5. Once determined _____ is safe, staff will sit with _____ and give reminders of appropriate ways to gain

attention from someone. Staff will explain _____ why self-injury is dangerous and ask _____to repeat an appropriate means of coping, such as, breathing exercises, talking with staff, taking a break, or switching activities.

6.   Staff will consult with psychologist or psychiatrist if _____ continues to exhibit self-injurious behavior or the severity of the behavior increases.

PERSEVERATING

Definition of the Behavior

Perseverating is defined as _____ continuing to dwell on subject matter that has already discussed. Typically _____ will continue to ask questions about the subject, sometimes repeating questions that have already been answered, talking about it incessantly, or demanding a response from staff when one has already been given. For _____, this is most frequently in regards to shopping activities or upcoming holidays and decorating.

*Count as a separate incident whenever there are at least ten minutes of calm between questions/demands/repetitive conversations.

Support Plan

1. Staff will remind _____ how to make plans at appropriate times and set aside time to discuss topics that he/she is persistently and repetitively asking about. Staff will remind _____ of

healthy ways to express anger, frustration, and sadness. Staff will encourage _____ to write or talk about his/her feelings with someone he/she feels most comfortable.

2. Staff will also remind _____ of basic relaxation training that consists of closing eyes, counting to 10, and thinking about a special place, and slowly opening and closing fingers on the hands. Staff will practice this training at least once each week.

3. If _____ appears to be fixating on something, staff will ask what is bothering him/her. If _____does not want to talk about it, staff will let him/her know to come to them when ready to talk. Staff will tell _____ that they can better help when he/she is open with them about feelings.

4. Staff will set aside time once a day for at least 10 minutes to talk with _____ 1:1 about any issues wished to be discussed. Staff will let _____ know that this is the time to plan/talk/ask staff about any issues because later they may not be available to do so.

Intervention Plan

1. If _____ begins to become obsessive about a topic, for example, asking repetitive questions that have already been answered, staff will immediately prompt to stop. Staff to let _____ know they will talk about it at a later time. Staff will remind _____ that this has already been talked about or answered.

2. Staff will remind _____ they have already answered this question or addressed the topic in some way. Staff will ask _____ to repeat the answer they have already given. When _____ responds correctly staff will say that is correct and to please follow the plan as discussed.

3. If _____ continues to perseverate about the issue staff will remind _____ that obsessive behavior is unhealthy. Staff will tell _____ to try to calm down, think about something else, and allow time to be alone if chooses to do so.

4. If _____ continues to talk incessantly about the subject and fixating on the issue staff will attempt to redirect to an activity that requires full attention. When appropriate, staff will engage in the redirection activity with _____, with reminders to stay focused on the task at hand.

5. If _____ continues to perseverate about an issue and refuses redirection staff will say they are going to walk away from the conversation and pay no additional attention. Staff will remind _____ to come and talk to them about another topic.

6. If _____ stops perseverating on an issue staff will give verbal praise for efforts to change the behavior and immediately reinforce with verbal praise and attention. Staff will tell _____ they appreciate his/her ability to stay on task and to regulate the behavior. Staff will remind _____ he/she is doing well and making progress in this area.

7. Staff will consult with psychologist or psychiatrist if _____ continues to exhibit fixating or obsessive behavior.

FREEZING/STARING

<u>Definition of the Behavior</u>

Freezing or staring behavior is defined as _____ becoming silent and staring directly at a person or down at an object ignoring the person talking while pretending as if unable to hear. This behavior is an antecedent to physical aggression. _____ will shut down and attempt to process information and feelings before striking at others. Staff are always instructed to back away when _____ begins freezing.

*Count as one incident every time _____ shuts down or freezes.

<u>Support Plan</u>

1. Facility staff will attempt to involve _____ in a variety of activities. Whenever possible, staff will offer a choice of times in which _____ can interact directly with staff and/or peers.

110

2. Staff will verbally praise and remind _____ that they are proud of him/her whenever participating in an activity and acting appropriately.

3. Staff will help _____ learn to communicate appropriately by identifying the freezing/staring behavior and explaining why he/she should signal others that some time is needed to calm down just before freezing. Staff will remind _____ other people may feel uncomfortable when staring at them and that people cannot understand when already frozen or refusing to speak.

4. Staff will have ongoing conversations with _____ about how others might interpret the freezing, or staring, behavior as intimidating or resistive behavior. During the conversation staff will remind _____ that the next step in behavioral progress is being able to signal or verbally inform others that a break is needed or time to think instead of simply freezing. Staff will encourage _____ to try and remember this and indicate to them next time.

5. Staff should help _____ to brainstorm different ways to communicate to others that he/she does not want to listen to what they have to say or that they are bothering him. This can include having _____ practice calmly telling someone that he/she is interested or that a minute is needed alone before addressing the issue. Staff will role play these situations with _____ for better practice.

Intervention Plan

1. If _____ begins to freeze, or stare, staff should immediately direct the person away from him. Staff should prompt _____ once to try and stop staring and continue with the activity at hand.

2. If continues staring, staff should tell _____ they know he/she is upset or overwhelmed right now, but that shutting down

is not the proper way to deal with the problem. Staff will tell _____ they are backing away and giving time to think about the situation. When ready he/she can come and join the group. Staff will not prompt _____ further for any reason.

3. At this time, staff will NO LONGER prompt _____. In the past over-prompting has escalated _____ to engage in physical aggression and property destruction which resulted in staff injury and destroyed property. Staff will remind _____ peers and any nearby staff to provide _____ with space for as much time as needed.

4. Later when _____ has returned to the group staff will praise the ability to calm self and return to the activity. Staff will remind _____ that a good job was done while not escalating the behavior. If _____ stops freezing/staring staff will reward with verbal praise and thanks for responding appropriately. For example, "Thank you _____ for turning that around! That was really awesome. Now let's have a good day together!"

5. Staff will continue ongoing conversations with _____ and with reminders of the next steps for progress. Such as, is informing people time away from the group is needed to calm down. Staff will encourage _____ to let them know when he/she does want to talk and when upset about something.

PHYSICAL AGGRESSION
INTENT TO HARM

Definition of the Behavior

Physical aggression is defined as anytime _____ takes an action with the intent to cause injury. For example; hitting, punching, pushing, kicking, scratching, and shoving. _____ has a history of violent physical aggression becoming upset especially when over-prompted. In the past _____ has caused injury to others resulting in bruising and requiring first aid.

*Staff will count as a separate incident every time there is an act of physical aggression or an attempt made.

Support Plan

1. Facility staff will attempt to involve _____ in a variety of activities. Whenever possible, staff will offer _____ a choice

of activities. During activities and when _____ is in a positive mood staff will have ongoing conversations about the importance of respecting others when they cannot do want we want.

2. Staff will also remind _____ that violence will never get what is wanted. Staff will explain, in order to help, he/she should approach others with a positive attitude and with respect. Staff will role play with _____ situations requiring a positive attitude and how to approach others with respect.

3. Staff will verbally praise and remind _____ they are proud whenever he/she participates in an activity and acts appropriately.

4. If _____ states that he/she does not want to participate in an activity staff should suggest participating at another time.

5. If _____ needs to participate in the activity at that time, staff will indicate why it is important to participate in the activity at that time.

6. Staff will not prompt _____ more than twice, to participate. Instead staff will not pay any additional attention to _____. Staff will verbally praise one of _____'s peers who are responding appropriately.

7. If _____ seems upset, staff will offer to talk about it. Staff will ask if something is bothering him/her. Staff will suggest that he/she might feel better if he/she talked about the problem.

8. If _____ does not want to talk, staff will not pursue the issue. Staff will suggest going someplace quiet, such as the bedroom or the back yard to calm down. Staff will suggest an alternative activity to help feel better, such as listening to music or drawing. Staff will always ask what is needed to feel better.

Intervention Plan

1. If _____ becomes physically aggressive, staff will firmly prompt to stop. Staff will remind _____ that violence is not the answer and they want to help.

2. While prompting _____ to stop, staff will direct away from others. Staff will also prompt _____'s peers to walk away and give _____ space and time to calm down.

3. If _____ continues to be physically aggressive, and if his behavior becomes dangerous to others, staff will immediately evacuate the area. Staff will tell _____ they are giving time and space to calm down.

4. If _____ continues the attempts to hurt someone, staff will motion to another staff to call the police. Staff should never say this out loud, instead use a code (not 911), if necessary. In the past mentioning the police, or 911, caused _____ to become more aggressive. If _____ is calm and the police arrive staff should ask the police to talk with _____ about the seriousness of the aggressive actions.

5. Staff will carefully document each time the physical aggression was dangerous to someone. Staff will indicate the following:

   a) Date and time that the dangerous behavior occurred

   b) A description of _____'s behavior that required serious intervention to stop injury

   c) A description of redirection attempted before injury occurred

   d) Staff person who had to intervene to prevent injury

   e) Staff person witnessing the intervention

6. Once _____ has been calm and not physically aggressive, for 10 minutes, staff will try to talk about the incident. Staff will encourage conversation about what was upsetting and caused anger.

7. Staff will help _____ determine more appropriate ways to handle anger and frustration next time something is upsetting. Staff will remind _____ that violence is never appropriate and that people cannot help get what is wanted if he/she is physically aggressive.

8. Staff will ask _____ if there is something he/she would like to say to the person that he/she was physically aggressive towards. Staff will never attempt to force _____ to apologize to the other person.

TAKING OTHER'S BELONGINGS

Definition of the Behavior

This behavior is defined as anytime _____ takes items that do not belong to him/her or takes an item from a store without paying it. _____ will typically take items from his/her peers, from staff or even facility supplies. _____ loves to make purchases but sometimes does not have money and this presents a risk in the community.

*Staff will count as a separate incident every time there is a separate item taken.

Support Plan

1. Staff will praise _____ frequently when he/she has not taken something that belongs to others. Staff will say, "_____ I'm really proud that you kept your hands to yourself

and used your own items today. You should also be proud of your progress in this area."

2. When _____ is in the facility staff will attempt to monitor closely making sure that valuable items are put away, along with food/lunch pails and magazines. If _____ seems to be 'eyeing' something staff should remove the item from view in an attempt to discourage feelings of desire to obtain the item.

3. From time to time staff will sit down with _____ and go over the facility rules and boundaries which include not going into others lunch pails/purses. Staff will remind _____ it is not okay to take things from a store without paying for them. Staff will inform _____ that this is against the law and could result in being arrested by the police.

4. Staff will monitor _____ even more closely when out in the community to ensure there is no opportunity to steal. Staff will remind _____ before entering a store to keep his/her hands to him/herself and that he/she has been doing well in this area of personal growth.

5. Staff will remind _____ that if he/she wants something he/she needs to ask for it or save money to buy it. Staff should offer to help budget/count money and teach how much money it take to purchase an item of choice.

6. Staff will remind _____ of the potential consequences of stealing through ongoing conversations and role play future situations with him/her. Staff will remind _____ what it feel like to have things stolen from him/her.

Intervention Plan

1. When an item is missing, staff will ask _____ is he/she has the item. If indicates he/she has it, staff will praise him/her for honesty, ask to return the item, and ask to think about an

apologizing to the person the item was taken from. Staff will never force _____ to apologize but remind him/her of how it helps to take responsibility for what we have done.

2. If _____ states he/she has not taken the item, staff will ask once more after a few minutes have passed. If _____ still claims he/she did not take the items staff will say okay and remind _____ that if the item is seen somewhere he/she should place the item on the table or at the front desk so that the owner might have it back.

3. If staff has seen that _____ took the item and he/she is still denying having taken it staff will remind him/her that by giving the item back he/she will not be in trouble. If _____ keeps the item and it is of significant value staff will remind _____ that he/she may have a meeting with his/her caseworker and repay his/her peer for the item taken.

4. Staff will explain to _____ why it is not appropriate to take things from others and ask how he/she would feel if things were taken from him/her.

5. In the event _____ returns with an item taken from a store, staff will attempt to take him/her back to the store to either return it or pay for it. If _____ refuses, staff will remind him/her they will have to return the item. Staff will ask _____ to forfeit the item to them.

6. Staff will always remind _____ that stealing in the community is illegal and that it can lead to being arrested and even receiving jail time. Staff will also tell _____ if they know he/she is continuing to steal while in the community and refusing to take the item back, the program rule that it is no longer appropriate to go on outings to shop in the community.

7. Staff will document each incident an item was stolen either from a store or from a peer/staff. Staff will list all of the newly acquired items and review during scheduled meetings with the caseworker in an attempt to determine how appropriate it is for _____ to

continue involvement in community shopping activities or how appropriate to repay a person for the items taken.

PROPERTY MISUSE
DESTRUCTION

<u>Definition of the Behavior</u>

Property misuse or destruction is defined anytime _____ misuses property by breaking, dropping, throwing or destroying it. _____ will bang fists or items on tables, windows, walls, or kick walls and doors. _____ will misuse or destroy his/her own property, typically clothing by chewing on it or pulling strings until it unravels and tearing it into pieces. Often this behavior is accompanied by screaming very loudly or making other screeching verbalizations. This behavior can last from a single incident to several minutes in length (5-10 minutes) if not successfully redirected.

*Staff will count as a single incident every time there is a separate destructive action made or item destroyed/misused.

<u>Support Plan</u>

1. Staff will involve _____ in cooperative activities with peers. Staff will attempt to involve _____ in games and crafts that require working cooperatively with others.

2. Staff will praise _____ for appropriate behavior and when working cooperatively with peers. Staff will particularly praise when property is being treated with care.

3. Staff will be aware when _____ appears to be angry or upset with someone. When aware of any facial expressions or body language that indicates escalation, staff will direct _____ away from the person or situation that is causing the upset. Staff will tell _____ they see he/she looks upset and would like to give a chance to get away from whatever is upsetting to allow time to calm down.

4. Staff will verbally praise _____ for walking away from the situation that seems to have been upsetting. If _____ does not want to walk away, staff will try to direct all attention towards an activity that is enjoyable. Staff will then praise _____ for walking away.

5. Staff will always phrase things positively. Staff will always make this a positive opportunity for _____ to treat property nicely and calmly.

Intervention Plan

1. If attempts to misuse property occurs, staff will verbally prompt _____ to stop. Staff will also attempt to direct away from the property.

2. If _____ continues the outburst, and then destroys property, staff will wait until calm for at least 15 minutes before addressing it.

3. Staff will remind _____ they understand he/she was upset. However, staff will also remind _____ that this behavior was not appropriate.

4. Once _____ has been calm for 15 minutes, staff will ask, when appropriate, to clean up any damage that has been caused. Staff will offer to assist _____ in doing so.

5. If _____ refuses to clean up, staff will only prompt twice, explaining it is necessary to be responsible for one's own emotions. Staff will not prompt a third time to clean up so as to not provoke frustration again.

6. If _____ destroys property and still refuses to help staff clean up, staff will ask one of a peer for their help. Staff will then verbally praise _____'s peer for helping by thanking them for their assistance and appropriate behavior.

7. If _____ has destroyed a peer's personal property staff should inform the program case manager. When determined appropriate _____ should repay the price of the personal property to the peer.

EXCESSIVE PHONE USE

Definition of the Behavior

Inappropriate and excessive phone use is defined as _____ continuously calling others over and over. _____ will call the service coordinator and the facility administrator excessively when upset about something. _____ will call peers, former boy/girlfriends, anyone where he/she has obtained a phone number. _____ may make verbal threats while requesting money and other items while on the phone. Historically, _____ has acted upon these threats but has not done so since being placed at his current home.

*Count as a separate incident whenever there are 10 minutes between episodes.

Support Plan

1. At random times, verbally praise appropriate social behavior.

Tell _____ you appreciate how well he/she is doing.

2. Staff will attempt to involve _____ in a variety of facility activities. Whenever possible staff will offer _____ choices between these activities.

3. Periodically throughout the day, staff will sit with _____ and attempt to engage in activities with him/her. Always try to give individual attention when behaving appropriately and not when he/she has done something inappropriate.

4. _____ should be given a special outing once a week when he/she has not displayed any negative behaviors for that week. This time should be given to _____ in order to have 1:1 attention. This is also a time for _____ to talk about feelings.

5. If there is a problem and _____ is asking to call the administrator and/or service coordinator, staff will explain a call can be made two times a week to service coordinator of if there is an emergency. A call to the administrator can be made one time a day. If unable to reach them _____ will be encouraged to leave a message and wait for a return call.

6. Staff will redirect _____'s attention to a different activity.

7. The administrator will set aside time each week to talk with _____ about his/her needs.

Intervention Plan

1. If _____ begins using the phone excessively staff will attempt to get _____ involved in a different activity such as going for a walk or helping staff with daily tasks around the facility.

2. Staff will remind _____ that excessive phone calls will not be answered. _____ can resolve concerns with staff first

before making outside calls for immediate needs.

3. Staff should also remind _____ of the reward which will be earned if appropriate behavior is displayed.

4. Once _____ has stopped using the phone excessively staff will verbally praise and let _____ know that they appreciate all efforts to make the right decision.

MAKING DEMANDS
BOSSING OTHERS

Definition of the Behavior

_____ often makes demands of staff and other consumers or bosses them around. _____ will often raise his/her voice, yelling directions at others in order to get them to do something for him/her or to control others. _____ is most likely to exhibit this behavior when resisting a task or does not want to participate. _____ may also exhibit this behavior when around peers and is not otherwise engaged in an activity of interest.

Support Plan

1. Staff will always offer _____ choices of activities and tasks. Staff will also try to be as flexible, as possible, with _____. An example would be offering _____ a choice of activities _____ likes for the completion of _____'s work duties. Staff will verbally praise _____ at various times when they observe socially positive and appropriate behavior with

127

peers. Staff will let _____ know how much they appreciate him/her being supportive and helpful towards others.

2. When requesting _____ to do something, staff will make requests in calm yet firm tone. Staff will try to gain _____'s eye contact when they talk with _____.

3. Staff will verbally praise _____ when being a leader and acting in a mature manner. Staff will praise _____ when they observe kindness to others. Staff will also encourage _____ to talk about any problems or concerns he/she may be experiencing with someone else. Staff will remind _____ it is the best way to solve problems.

4. Staff will periodically explain to _____ the importance of attending to his/her own job duties and tasks and not interrupt others while working, telling others what to do, or being bossy to peers. Staff will verbally praise _____ for doing own work, talking nicely to others, and not interrupting others while they work.

Intervention Plan

1. When requesting _____ to do something, staff will make requests in calm yet firm tone. Staff will try to gain _____'s eye contact when they talk with _____.

2. Staff will verbally praise _____ when being a leader and acting in a mature manner. Staff will praise _____ when they observe kindness to others. Staff will also encourage _____ to talk about any problems or concerns he/she may be experiencing with someone else. Staff will remind _____ it is the best way to solve problems.

3. Staff will periodically explain to _____ the importance of attending to his/her own job duties and tasks and not interrupt others while working, telling others what to do, or being bossy to

peers. Staff will verbally praise _____ for doing own work, talking nicely to others, and not interrupting others while they work.

4. When providing _____ a directive or making a request, staff will use effective cueing procedures and immediately turn and walk away or turn attention to another task. Periodically staff will return to _____ and prompt again. Staff will not linger to hear _____'s bossy complaints, demands, or arguing. Walking away helps to avoid being drawn into _____'s delay tactics and need for attention. It is very easy to be drawn into the behavior. Once this is realized, staff should stop responding immediately, turn, and walk away.

Examples of effective cues:

Calmly saying, "Please do you own work" or "Please stop bossing others and pay attention to your own work", rather than excitedly saying, "STOP BEING BOSSY!"

Walking over to _____ and pointing to a symbol for being kind or cooperative, such as a happy face, rather than loudly saying across the room, "Stop bossing others!"

5. If _____ does not respond to a request to stop being bossy or demanding within 5 minutes, staff will ask once more, reminding him/her that they would appreciate help or need him/her to complete a task with them.

6. Staff will explain the importance of _____'s participation in doing an activity or job assignment. Staff will always ask _____ if he/she understands their reasoning and what his/her thoughts/feelings are about it.

7. If _____ continues to ignore the request, staff will ask one of _____'s peers to complete a request. Staff will praise that peer for following that request.

8. Staff will return about 10 minutes later and talk to _____ about the situation. Staff will tell_____ they know that sometimes he/she may not want to do something or feels the need to tell others what to do. Staff to remind _____they are there to help others learn and stay on task.

9. Staff will positively reinforce _____ with verbal praise when compliant and responding appropriately. For example, "_____, thank you for helping us and not worrying about what others are doing" or "I appreciate it when you are nice to others and not bossy."

TEASING
HORSEPLAY

Definition of the Behavior

Teasing or horse playing is defined as anytime _____ teases others about something or purposely bothers another about an issue to annoy or agitate them. _____taunts others and plays a practical jokes.

Support Plan

1. Staff will attempt to involve _____ in a variety of activities. Whenever possible, staff will offer _____ a choice between times in which he/she can complete work alone or participate in a group activity.

2. Staff will verbally praise _____ and remind him/her they are proud of him/her, whenever participating in an activity and acting appropriately.

3. Staff will help _____ learn to communicate appropriately

by identifying the teasing behavior and explaining why it is wrong and hurtful to others.

4. From time to time staff will role play situations with _____ in an attempt to convey and help him/her feel empathy. Staff will remind _____ that if we treat others with respect they will treat us with respect.

Intervention Plan

1. If _____ becomes inappropriate by teasing others or purposely bothering them, staff will firmly prompt him/her to stop. Staff will remind _____ one of the goals is to stop engaging in this behavior.

2. While prompting _____ to stop, staff will direct away from others. Staff will prompt _____'s peers to walk away and allow space and time to change his/her attitude.

3. If _____ continues to be communicating inappropriately, and if the behavior becomes hurtful to others, staff will tell _____ not to take his/her anger out on others and not to say mean things.

4. Once _____ has been calm and communicating appropriately for 10 minutes, staff will try to talk about the incident. Staff will encourage conversation about why the teasing of others began and practice the role playing exercise.

5. Staff will help _____ determine more appropriate things that can be done the next time he/she becomes upset about something or feels the need for attention, such as breathing exercises or coming to staff first with concerns.

6. Staff should also ask _____ if there is something he/she would like to say to the person being teased or bothered. Staff will

never attempt to force _____ to apologize to the other person.

MIMICKING OTHERS

Definition of the Behavior

Behavioral mimicking is defined as copying the behaviors of others, often when they change behaviors or repeating words and phrases said by other to gain attention. _____ has a history of copying peers when they do something that receives staff redirection or attention of some kind. This includes _____ incessantly interrupting, clapping over and over again, making loud noises, chirping, screaming, moving/pushing/shifting furniture back and forth/towards people, slamming doors, running down the hallway or in an activity room or community location (fast food restaurant, store). This behavior might also include physical aggression with poking, kicking others, or hitting them. All of these behaviors are a direct copycat like production in that _____ will be conducting him/herself appropriately until he/she sees or hears someone doing something that receives attention. Then, he/she will mimic the behavior or sounds exactly. This behavior can last anywhere from a single mimicked gesture or word to several mimicked actions or phrases repeated incessantly.

*Staff will count as one incident every time there is at least ten minutes of calm between episodes of behavioral mimicking.

Support Plan

1. Staff will talk to _____to determine if he/she is receiving enough attention and is in a positive emotional state. Staff will occasionally check in with _____ and ask how he/she is feeling. Whenever possible, staff will give the opportunity to talk with them 1:1. Staff will always make _____ aware of the amount of time they have, so to avoid provocation by staff's inability to spend large amounts of time 1:1.

2. Staff will work with _____ and another peer in order to promote the ability to work cooperatively with peers without copying their behaviors or phrases by providing attention when acting appropriately and asking questions directed to him/her while waiting for an answer. Staff will prompt _____ to stop copying and wait for the peer to finish answering their question.

3. Staff will involve _____ in a variety of activities. Whenever possible, staff will offer _____ a choice between times in which he/she can interact directly with just staff or peers, separately or altogether in a group. Staff will verbally praise _____ and remind him/her of being proud whenever participating in an activity and acting appropriately.

4. Staff will attempt to schedule as much physical activity or exercise, as possible. If applicable, this should take place in the morning or prior to activities that require _____ to sit for long periods of time in order to expend _____'s emotional energy and optimize compliance/non-copying.

5. Staff will have ongoing conversations with _____ that include explanations why it is rude to copy others and that doing so could escalate a peer's behavior. Staff will remind _____ that others do not appreciate when _____ does this and may not want to be around him/her as a result.

6. Staff will remind _____ that he/she should think about the golden rule "treat others how you would like to be treated." they will remind _____ that he/she would not appreciate of others were to point out things he/she has done wrong.

Intervention Plan

1. If _____ begins mimicking or copying others, staff will immediately prompt _____ to stop and remind _____ of being socially inappropriate. For example staff may say, "_____, stop copying that's not nice. It is rude to imitate others" or "_____ stop. Remember, it is not appropriate to copy the changing behavior of others." Staff will attempt to explain the actions appear to be rude to others as they are socially inappropriate and can be viewed as teasing or making fun of someone. Staff will remind _____ that peers may not want to be around when he/she is engaging in this behavior and that he/she might become the target of their changing behavior creating an unsafe situation for him/her.

2. If it is necessary for staff to confront _____ about changing behavior, they will use a calm, firm tone that will not provoke _____ to act out. Staff will remember they should direct their comments to _____ but be short and to the point as he/she will often exhibit this behavior for attention. Staff will firmly prompt _____ to stop while using a calm and low tone of voice. Staff should be aware that yelling or using high pitched voice is likely to add to the hyperactivity or escalate the behavior.

3. If _____ changes the subject when staff is confronting him/her about a behavior, staff will tell _____ they do not like when he/she tries to change the subject. Staff will remind _____ that it is okay to tell them when upset or needing attention. At this time, staff will also direct _____ away from others. Staff will prompt _____'s peers to walk away and give space and time to change his/her attitude. Staff will remind _____ that his/her peers do not wish to be around

when being treated with disrespect.

4. If _____ continues mimicking behavior by copying, teasing, or repeating others, staff will firmly prompt him/her to stop. Staff will remind _____ that one of the goals is to stop engaging in this behavior. Staff will remind _____ they are the staff and it is their job to handle the situation. Staff will then ignore ongoing behavior for the time being and only say to her, "_____ you know that you should not be copying others, I'm going to disengage from you until you can stop copying and talk appropriately." Staff will then disengage and interact with one of the nearby peers who are acting appropriately.

5. Staff will praise _____ when not engaging in mimicking behavior and tell him/her they really appreciate it when treating peers with respect.

6. If _____ continues to mimic, copy or repeat the actions/phrases of peers and the behavior becomes hurtful to others, staff will tell _____ that his/her peers do not want to be copied. While prompting _____ to stop, staff will prompt _____'s peers to walk away and give space and time to calm down; ignoring _____ if they have to. Staff will remember that this behavior can trigger peer changing behavior and further escalate _____. Separating the two is essential to de-escalating the situation.

7. Staff will talk with _____ privately with reminders it is not the time to copy or mimic peers. Staff will remind _____ that following directions now will help him/her to continue to be successful throughout the day. If _____ is continuing the behavior, staff will inform _____ that they plan to disengage. Staff may say, "Okay _____, it seems that you need some time and space away from me to calm down. I am now going to disengage until you can compose yourself. When you are calm, ready, and done copying others, you may come back to me and the group to complete an activity.

8. At this time staff will pay no additional attention to _____ or the behavior. Staff will attempt to keep peers focused on the activity while not making eye contact but still monitoring his/her person from a distance. Staff will continue this until _____ has ceased engaging in mimicking.

9. Once _____ has been calm and not mimicking others for at least 5 minutes and if _____ comes back to the group staff will positively reinforce his/her ability to do so by using verbal praise and light physical touch, such as a high five or a pat on the back. Staff may say, "_____ you did such a good job calming down and I really appreciate your ability to do so."

10. Staff will help _____ determine more appropriate things that can be done or said the next time he/she wants or needs attention. Staff will help _____ to remember some phrases to be used instead, such as, "Can you please spend some time with me?" or "I am feeling left out." Staff will encourage _____ to come to them and let them know when he/she wants attention and will remind _____ that they want to give that attention but that copying inappropriate phrases or changing behavior will not help get what is wanted.

DISROBING
UNDRESSING

Definition of the Behavior

Disrobing or undressing is defined as _____ purposely taking off clothing at inappropriate times. _____ will do this at home, day program, or the community.

*Staff will count as a separate episode whenever there are separate actions of undressing that take place.

Support Plan

1. Staff will always try to offer _____ choices of activities and tasks by physically showing two possibilities and asking which activity is preferred. Staff will attempt to keep _____

engaged and physically active throughout the day. Staff will be as flexible as possible with _____ by not forcing one activity over another.

2. Staff will also allow _____ to choose to change clothing sometime during the day if possible. Staff should encourage house staff to provide a spare clothing item for _____ to change into when he/she wants or needs to change clothing throughout the day.

3. If _____ spills something on clothing staff will clean the spot so that _____ will not focus on his clothing. If it cannot be cleaned without washing and it noticeably bothers _____ staff should ask if he/she would like to change clothes.

4. When making a request of _____, staff will attempt to use calm and inviting gestures. Staff will establish eye contact with _____ when working together to make sure it is understood what is being asked.

Intervention Plan

1. When _____ begins taking off clothing staff will immediately prompt to stop in a calm but firm voice. Staff will remind _____ that taking off clothing in the middle of the program area is never appropriate.

2. If _____ does not respond to a request to stop disrobing within 1 minute, staff will gently help _____ back into the clothing item or hold the clothing item so that it is understood the item of clothing needs to be kept on.

3. Staff will prompt _____ to go to the restroom if he/she wishes to disrobe. Staff will attempt to gently guide _____ away from his peers and toward the restroom while continuing to prompt to keep the clothing on.

4. If _____ forces the clothing off even after staff attempts to keep them on, staff will leave _____ alone for one minute and direct peers away from him/her. Staff will immediately return and prompt _____ to put the clothes back on by handing them back and helping _____ back into the clothing.

5. When _____ complies with keeping the clothing on, or puts the clothing back on after taking them off, staff will verbally praise _____ for doing so. Staff will remind _____ they appreciate when he/she listens to directions and acts appropriately.

INAPPROPRIATE TOUCHING OF OTHERS

Definition of the Behavior

Inappropriate touching is defined as _____ hugging staff from behind, touching, grabbing, tickling, or hugging around the chest/breast area. _____ may continue attempting to grab or touch male/female staff even after having been asked to stop. _____ does not exhibit this behavior while out in the community. _____ may display this behavior when trying to get the attention of staff or when seated close to someone. _____ does not seem to have personal boundaries at times and will get too close to others when speaking potentially leading to grabbing behavior.

*Count as a separate incident whenever there are 10 minutes between episodes. Also include any attempts.

Support Plan

1. Staff should be sure they model appropriate behavior throughout the day.

2. Staff should be sure they maintain an appropriate professional relationship with firm boundaries.

3. When interacting with _____ staff should maintain personal space at all times.

4. Staff should not hug _____. When greeting _____ staff will give a high five or handshake. Staff will role play with _____ to model appropriate social behavior on a daily basis.

5. Staff will periodically remind others about personal space. Staff will do this in a group setting being certain specific individuals are not targeted, but discuss this with the group as a whole. Staff will also role play appropriate social behavior with the group and discuss why it is important to have good social skills in the facility and community.

Intervention Plan

1. If _____ touches someone inappropriately staff should immediately ask to stop and try to redirect attention to a different activity.

2. Staff should do this while keeping a distance so there is no touching of others inappropriately.

3. If staff sees _____ inappropriately touching another peer staff will immediately ask to stop. If _____ does not stop staff will give a reminder that this is a form of harassment and _____ needs to respect the space of others.

4. Staff will remind _____ about appropriate boundaries.

5. Staff will redirect the peer and _____'s attention elsewhere, preferably away from each other. If the situation persists staff should utilize their CPI techniques to ensure consumer safety. Staff should utilize the least restrictive methods first and only escalate the efforts until the behaviors have ceased. If any restrictive methods are used, staff should inform the administrator immediately and document the incident.

6. Staff will remind others as a group when everyone is calm about respecting each other's personal space and talk about why this is important, while not addressing _____ individually.

THREATS OF SUICIDE

<u>Definition of the Behavior</u>

Threats of suicide is defined as _____ making statements that _____'s life is not worth living, that he/she wants to die, or that he/she wants to kill him/herself. _____ has a long history of making suicidal statements and may act upon these threats. _____ has taken butter knives out of the drawers from previous homes and threatened to kill him/herself.

*Count as a separate incident each time _____ makes a suicidal statement or attempts to hurt self.

<u>Support Plan</u>

1. Staff will periodically counsel _____ throughout the day to see how he/she is feeling.

2. Staff should help _____ generate a list of activities enjoyed and arrange for opportunities to participate in these

145

activities. Staff should help _____ keep an active schedule to avoid unstructured time. This will help _____ keep his/her mind involved in productive activities.

3. Staff will provide _____ 1:1 time throughout the day and engage _____ in conversations. Staff will assess _____'s mood and encourage socialization with others, doing tasks around the facility, and participating in recreational activities with staff or peers.

4. If _____ appears to be upset, staff will ask if he/she wants to talk about the situation. Staff will to listen to _____, to help self-esteem, mood, and feeling better overall.

5. If _____ does not want to talk, staff will suggest participation in a preferred activity, such as, watching TV with his peers, playing a game, or getting some fresh air outside. _____ also enjoys listening to music and watching television and may be encouraged to do so. _____ may also write his/her feelings down in a journal and share them with staff when ready to talk.

6. Staff will carefully scan the facility on a regular basis for any objects that are possibly dangerous or sharp to ensure _____ does not have the opportunity to hurt self.

7. Staff will monitor _____ throughout the day to ensure not too much time is spent isolated in a room.

Intervention Plan

1. If _____ starts to make suicidal statements, staff will strongly prompt to stop. Staff will ask if there is anything that he/she would like to talk about.

2. Staff will encourage _____ to participate in an activity of

choice (playing a game, watching TV, listening to music, etc.) and will not leave _____ alone until they feel his/her mood has improved.

3. Staff may encourage _____ to spend time in bedroom but also encourage _____ to leave the door open so that staff may monitor his/her well-being for safety precautions. Staff should never lose sight of _____ once stated he/she wants to hurt self.

4. Staff will remind _____ that he/she is important to them and that nothing will be solved with attempting to hurt self.

5. Staff will ask _____ how he/she would attempt to commit suicide. If the plan is realistic staff to discuss further and contact the facility administrator or mental health professional immediately.

6. If _____ is found attempting to commit suicide staff will implement crisis intervention techniques and document the incident according to facility procedures as a special incident. Staff must also notify the appropriate agencies.

7. Staff will talk with _____ about how he/she is feeling and help problem solve as to what solutions will benefit him/her instead of attempting self-injury or suicide.

TOILETING ACCIDENTS

Definition of the Behavior

Toileting accidents are primarily defined as _____ having bowel movements and bladder accidents outside the toilet area. _____ at times sits hard on the toilet causing it to lift up. Toilet water and feces may spill out onto the floor. _____ may also defecate on self and track feces throughout the home. _____ may laugh before displaying this behavior.

*Count as a separate incident for each time _____ has a toileting accident.

Support Plan

1. Staff will continue to teach _____ how to properly use the restroom by utilizing effective toileting practices through positive reinforcement.

2. Staff will also continue to monitor _____ while he/she is in the restroom to ensure that wiping is thorough. Staff will

remind _____ of the importance of good hygiene and verbally praise whenever he/she complies with good hygiene and grooming practices.

3. Staff will model how to gently sit on the toilet and encourage practice of how to do so when _____ does not need to use the restroom.

4. Staff will also remind _____ to use the restroom frequently throughout the day and give him/herself time to use it.

5. Staff will continue to encourage _____ not to drink excessive amounts of soda to improve health. Staff will remind _____ that he/she feels better and has fewer toileting accidents when maintaining a healthier diet.

6. Staff will also discuss with _____ that it is not alright to be incontinent on purpose. Staff will monitor _____ when laughing to him/herself and give reminders to use the toilet appropriately before entering the restroom.

Intervention Plan

1. Staff will continue to prompt _____ to clean up after self when a toileting accident occurs. Thank _____ for compliance.

2. Staff will tell _____ he/she is doing a great job every time using the restroom appropriately and praise for being mature and responsible. Staff will tell _____ how proud they are and reward with daily verbal praise and weekly rewards as determined by staff.

MASTURBATION

Definition of the Behavior

This is defined as touching self in front of others in public places. This may include attempts to touch others inappropriately. Typically _____ will put his/her hand down his/her pants and attempt to rub self or grab/pinch the butt of another person. Sometimes this includes making sexual gestures or kissing faces toward others while touching self on the outside of pants.

Count as a separate incident whenever there are separate actions made.

Support Plan

1. Staff will regularly engage _____ in scheduled activities. Whenever possible staff will offer _____ a choice between activities. Staff will involve _____ in making the program schedule by asking what preferred activities he/she would like to participate in for the upcoming week.

2. Staff will be as flexible as possible with _____ whenever planning activities but will keep _____ on task and engaged. For example; if _____ is refusing to participate in a craft activity, staff may ask for participation in a different activity, maybe a board game, in the same room as the proposed craft activity.

3. Staff will provide physical activity for _____ to engage in at least once a day for approximately 30 minutes to an hour. This might include a short walk around the block, stretching/weight lifting, or a Wii game.

4. Whenever _____ is behaving appropriately staff will positively reinforce _____ by saying things like, "Good job!" or "Thank you _____" in a high pitch voice or approving tone. Staff will thank _____ for keeping his/her hands out of pants when asked or when behaving appropriately without any prompts from staff.

5. From time to time when _____ completes a staff request or acts appropriately staff will give _____ appropriate physical contact such as a pat on the back, high fives, or a light touch on the arm. Staff will explain to _____ why these actions are appropriate physical touches. During this time staff should also explain that inappropriate sexual behavior in public is illegal and could result in being arrested.

6. Staff will remind _____ to put hand up for a high five or to offer a handshake to others when greeting them. Staff will remind _____ to keep his/her hands to self and outside of pants.

7. Staff will remind _____ they will respond to needs by observing when he/she wants something or is attempting to get someone's attention. Staff will tell _____ they will only respond to celebrate when acting appropriately.

Intervention Plan

1. If _____ attempts/begins to masturbate in front of others, staff will gently remind that he/she needs to finish this activity in private without other people observing. Staff will suggest the bathroom or wait until getting home. Staff will praise _____ for complying with that request.

2. If _____ continues to masturbate in front of others, staff will again direct to someplace private. Staff will suggest using the restroom and remind that a public or shared room is never an appropriate place to masturbate.

3. If _____ still continues to masturbate, staff will walk away for several minutes. Staff will direct any peers that are nearby, to another area. Staff will remind others not to observe this behavior and explain that it is inappropriate.

4. Staff will return several minutes later when _____ is no longer touching self and talk to _____ again about why that behavior is inappropriate. Staff will give reminders they want him/her to have privacy when engaging in this act and if chooses to do so in the restroom. Staff will explain that it makes others uncomfortable and that it is illegal to do in public. Staff will continue to explain the possible repercussions of engaging in the behavior in public.

5. If _____ attempts/begins to masturbate in public, staff will firmly prompt to stop and explain it is not appropriate at that time. Staff will immediately remind _____ of the legalities. When doing so staff will use a deep firm voice.

6. If _____ continues to masturbate in public or keep hands in pants, staff will gently touch on the arm and gesture to remove hands from pants. Staff to remind _____ they are attempting to save him/her from engaging in illegal behavior.

7. Staff may direct _____ to the nearest bathroom if having difficulty following staff requests while explaining the need for privacy while doing this. Staff will continue to explain the repercussions of public masturbation and how it could result in possible jail time.

8. Staff will have ongoing conversations with _____ regarding when and where this behavior is considered appropriate. Staff will discuss this in a positive and unemotional tone. Staff will always attempt to engage _____ in these conversations and ask if they are being understood by _____.

CHAPTER TWO

BEHAVIORAL TIPS AND TECHNIQUES

Behavior: Indication of a Medical Condition?

Behaviors are a form of communication particularly for someone who is unable to verbalize their hurt or pain. It is easy to misunderstand signs of a medical problem when observing a challenging behavior. We must observe and ask ourselves if a behavior is possibly caused by an underlying medical condition and be alert to non-verbal signs of communication.

<u>Self-Injurious Behavior</u>

Hand biting may be caused by dental pain. Chewing of the fingers may indicate nausea, indigestion, reflux, or local infection. Hitting or banging of the head may indicate headache, shunt problems, sinusitis, dental pain, eye, or possibly an ear infection.

General scratching and rubbing may be a misunderstood sign of eczema, scabies, lice, an insect bite, sunburn, or other skin conditions. It may indicate liver or kidney disease. Scratching and rubbing the abdomen may be indication of an ulcer, gastritis, gall bladder/pancreas problems or menstrual discomfort. If scratching and rubbing the chest is observed these may be non-verbal indications of pneumonia, indigestion, reflux, or even angina.

Constipation and hemorrhoids may be indicated by scratching and rubbing of the rectum.

Aggressive or Violent Behavior

General aggressive or violent behavior may be an indication of hypothyroidism, hyperthyroidism, temporal lobe seizures, caffeine or substance abuse, headache or infection.

Unusual Movements or Postures

Rocking may be an indication of back or hip pain, indigestion, or reflux. Visual problems, sinus infection or vertigo may be observed with head tilting or waving. Sitting may be seen when an individual is experiencing vertigo. Sudden sitting may indicate cardiac problems or seizures. Other unusual posture may mean limb fractures, hip pain, rectal pain or genital pain.

Recurrent Masturbation

Recurrent masturbation may indicate a urinary tract infection, vaginal infection or prostate inflammation.

Non-Compliant/Resistive Behavior

When giving a directive, an individual may pretend to be unaware they have been given a request. They may be aware but make no effort to comply. Often, there are attempts to change the conditions by making a deal, or arguing. There may be threats to hurt others, responses by saying "no", or revealed anger.

It is important to consistently provide effective cues which impact the amount of compliance to follow. A cue, must be given so it is clearly understood and sorted out by the individual. Once awareness has been obtained a cue must be offered without excess emotion. The expected reaction should be something that is attainable and realistic.

As reflected in the Positive Behavioral Support Plan templates provided, effective cues must be provided in three steps:

1. Verbal prompt

2. Visual prompt using a picture, sign, or gesture.

3. Physical prompt using a gentle touch or physical assistance.

After giving a directive, immediately turn and walk away or turn attention to something else. From time to time, return and repeat directive again. Do not linger to hear grievances, comments, or arguments. It is best to simply walk away without reacting. This helps to avoid delay tactics and other attempts at redirection. If drawn in, stop responding immediately, turn and walk away.

If the individual complies with the directive, support them with verbal praise or a gentle touch. Repeat this whenever compliance is practiced. Unfortunately, compliance rarely occurs in the early stages. Reinforcement, such as praise or something enjoyed, needs to be provided every time the individual complies. Once compliance becomes more frequent the reinforcement may be diminished to where it is no longer required for the entire activity.

It is important to understand the techniques of offering regular and frequent choices to empower an individual. Be flexible and avoid engaging in power struggles. It is sometimes difficult but never take resistive responses personally.

Decreasing Probability of Actions

Eliminate Enticements and Triggers

Frequently, objects or items in a setting may act as triggers to approach or engage the object. For example, to some individuals an open cabinet may be an invitation to sneak food. For others, pictures on the wall may be a cue to pull them down. These instances will most likely result in staff intervention. By eliminating these temptations the problem behaviors are likely to be eliminated and the need for staff intervention becomes unnecessary.

Adjust the Area and Surroundings

Many behavior problems are associated with specific arrangements of furniture or locations in a room. For example, young woman yells, screams and hits others only when she sits in a green chair pointed in a specific direction. By changing to a different color chair and its position, the behavior may be eliminated when not involved structured time.

Split Up and Reposition

Certain people simply do not get along with each other. They may touch, push, grab, and pull at each other. They may verbally or physically attack other as they come closer to them. By temporarily splitting them up, negative interactions that have potentially hazardous consequences may be prevented.

Adjust the Setting and Time of Activities

Serious behavior problems in certain situations and at select times may be exhibited by certain people. For example, hitting may occur only in the dining room but not in the kitchen. Tantrums may occur during activities presented just before breakfast. By changing the location and/or time of the activities challenging behaviors may not present themselves at all.

Chapter Three

Bringing Your Templates Together

Final Plans

The Positive Behavior Support Plans you create from the provided templates should include measureable goals. In addition to the plans, behavior charts and documentation should be completed to evaluate progress in meeting each objective.

Positive Behavior Support Plans consist of using the least amount of intervention possible while reinforcing appropriate alternative behaviors. The goal of a Positive Behavior Support Plan is to change, decrease, or extinguish a challenging behavior. Its success is measured by decreased challenging behaviors, increased performance of replacement skills, and improved quality of life.

SAMPLE COMPLETED REPORT

Name and Address of Company/School

Name of Individual - POSITIVE SUPPORT PLANS

Name: _____
BD: _____
Age: _____ years, _____ months
Date of Plans: _____
Written By: _____

BEHAVIORAL OBJECTIVES

Goal:

To reduce the frequency of challenging behaviors by 25% quarterly.

Targeted Behaviors:

The following challenging behaviors have been targeted for behavioral support:

(1) Physical Aggression
(2) False Allegations/Statements
(3) Inappropriate Sexual/Social Behavior

PHYSICAL AGGRESSION

Definition of the Behavior

Physical aggression is defined as any behavior exhibited toward someone else that has the potential to cause injury. In _____'s case this is grabbing others very tightly and clenching his/her fist very hard, often scratching people or digging in with his/her nails. On occasion _____ has pinched others and slapped/hit others when very agitated. Most often _____ is does not intend to hurt the person but attempting to get their attention or keep them from walking away. As a result of grabbing so hard this causes minor scratches or bruising on the person. In the past _____ has caused minor damage to others resulting in first aid while exhibiting this behavior.

*Count as a separate incident whenever there are separate acts of aggression.

Support Plan

(1) Staff will attempt to involve _____ in various activities. Staff will offer a choice between at least two activities whenever possible. Staff will ask, "_____, what would you like to do?" while showing at least two different choices in activities, exercise, crafts, or movies.

(2) Staff will always monitor _____'s interaction with his/her peers to make sure the interaction is appropriate and that his/her peers are not making fun or teasing _____ in some way.

(3) Staff should also be observant of _____'s mood by watching facial reactions and body language. If _____ seems to be upset or agitated staff should attempt to position his/her peers away so that _____ does not grab at them.

164

(4)   If _____ is upset or agitated during an activity that requires others to be close staff will attempt to calm _____ with their voice by using a calm and gentle tone saying, "_____ you're doing okay. Take a deep breath. We are almost done. I really appreciate you staying calm until we are finished."

(5)   If staff are prompting participation and _____does not respond after the first prompt, staff will wait at least 1 minute before making another prompt. At this time staff will continue to stand with/next to _____ allowing time to think and respond before walking away.

(6)   When _____ makes a choice, staff will help _____ begin the activity thanking him/her for participation. If _____ does not respond after 1 minute staff will let _____ know they are going to walk away to give time to think about the prompt. Staff will tell _____ where they are going to be so that when he/she is ready to come find staff. For example; "_____ would you like to watch a movie or complete a puzzle? Wait one minute for response. "Ok _____, I am going to finish cooking while you think about it. When you decide I will be in the kitchen and you can come to the kitchen to let me know what choice you have made."

(7)   Whenever _____ appears to be upset, staff will ask if he/she needs something or if they can help in some way. Staff might say, "_____ you look unhappy can I help you with something?" If _____ states what is wrong staff should attempt to remedy the situation. If the situation cannot be remedied or _____ continues to perseverate on the issue staff will attempt to redirect him/her into a preferred activity. Staff should do their best to give _____ a meaningful role in the activity or co-engage him/her in the activity.

Examples:

Redirection: "Well _____, I cannot change what happened at day program but I can help you complete (favorite activity) if you want."

Meaningful Task: "_____, I would really appreciate if you could help me. I need someone to call out the Bingo numbers for our Bingo game so that everyone can hear. Will you pick out and call the numbers?"

Engage Together – "Ok _____, I will put glue on the back of these and you can now stick it to the paper. Tell me when you want me to hand you another one with glue."

(8)   Staff will always attempt give _____ an appropriate amount of personal space, at least an arm's length of distance, between themselves and _____. Staff will also instruct _____'s peers to allow personal space when walking around him/her or working/sitting with him/her in a group.

(9)   Staff will periodically provide verbal praise to _____ when acting appropriately and is not physically aggressive. For example: "Good job _____" or "Thank you for coming to get me and tapping me softly." Staff will also smile and use light physical touch, such as, a pat on the back or shoulder or a high five.

(10)   Staff should have ongoing conversations with _____ that explain why holding on to people too hard is not appropriate. Staff will explain this can cause harm and can make people uncomfortable. Staff will also remind _____ how to get someone's attention appropriately in others ways, like calling their name, tapping them softly on the back or saying, "Excuse me" to the nearest person.

(11)   Staff will always attempt to make their whereabouts known
to _____ when they are in the house. Staff will remind
_____ they are always available to help meet his/her needs
and not to worry about them leaving. Staff will always wait for
_____ to finish his/her thoughts or sentences before walking
away and whenever possible remind _____ where they will
be.

Intervention Plan

(1)   If _____ is beginning to grab someone, staff will
remind him/her to be soft and not to grab for too long. If
_____ is already grabbing very hard staff will firmly prompt
him/her to stop. Staff will be firm but never harsh or scolding.
Staff will simply say, "_____ stop. You are grabbing too hard.
You are hurting the person." Staff will remind _____ that it is
important to be soft when getting the attention of others.

(2)   While prompting to stop, staff will direct _____
away from the person that he/she is being physically aggressive
toward. Staff to provide space between _____ and
themselves by backing up while still talking to him/her. Staff will
ensure there is enough space between the peer, themselves, and
_____. Staff to switch his focus of aggression toward them
in their attempts to redirect.

(3)   Staff will attempt to engage _____ in another
activity as part of the redirection. Staff will provide _____ at
least two choices of activity or craft. Staff to say, "_____,
let's come over here and do an activity. Would you like to draw or
would you like to complete this puzzle?"

(4)   Staff will also remind _____ to show or tell them
what is upsetting. Staff will always make themselves available to
talk with _____ about what is bothering him/her. Staff will
remind _____ that it is not okay to grab, hit, push or scratch

someone. Staff will remind _____ that when aggressive toward people they will not want to engage or be around him/her.

(5)   If staff attempts to involve _____ in an activity as part of the redirection and he/she becomes physically aggressive, or continues to be aggressive, staff will stop the activity for at least five minutes until he/she calms down. Staff will say, "_____ I am going to back away to give you space because you seem upset. Take some time to calm down and I will come back to you when you are calm and ready."

(6)   Staff will attempt to resume the activity once _____ has been calm and not attempted to be physically aggressive for at least five minutes. If _____ is no longer physically aggressive and chooses to engage in an activity staff will positively reinforce _____ with verbal praise regarding his/her ability to calm down and choose to behave appropriately.

FALSE ALLEGATIONS/STATEMENTS

Definition of the Behavior

False allegations or statements are defined as _____ making up stories or making comments about others that are untrue. For example, _____ will accuse his/her peers of "being real bad today". Staff asks how everyone is doing despite witnessing the peer being calm and appropriate all day. In the past _____ has made up stories about staff or activities that happened at day program that were verified as false.

*Count as a separate incident whenever there is a separate story/statement made.

Support Plan

(1)   Staff will attempt to talk to _____ periodically to ensure that enough attention is being received and that _____ is in a positive emotional state. For example staff might say, "How are you feeling today _____? Do you need some one on one time?" Staff will occasionally check in with _____ and ask how he/she is feeling. Whenever possible, staff will give _____ an opportunity to talk with them one on one. Staff will also encourage _____ to talk to them when something is bothering him/her and explain that if upset he/she may feel better by talking to staff.

(2)   Staff will always make _____ aware of the amount of time they have to spend with or engage in an activity so he/she is not provoked by staff's inability to spend large amounts of time with him/her one on one. Staff will provide _____ with a five minute warning before disengaging a conversation or activity to allow _____ adequate time to finish what is being said or done before the activity terminates.

(3)   Staff will always use a calm tone of voice when talking with _____ that will not provoke _____ to act out. Staff will remind _____ through the ongoing conversation they enjoy talking with him/her and appreciate him/her being honest with them. Staff will promote honesty on a normal basis with _____ by explaining the importance and how it directly links to being trustworthy. Staff will reward _____ for honesty and good behavior with verbal praise and one on one attention.

(4)   If _____ makes a claim that staff is not sure is true, staff will ask _____ if he/she is sure about what he/she is saying. Staff will let _____ know that they are not sure if the story is accurate and they are giving him/her a chance to change the story. Staff will remind _____ not to be afraid to tell the truth and they are there to help.

Intervention Plan

(1)   If _____ begins to make false statements, staff will tell _____ they appreciate honesty and feel as if he/she is currently being dishonest. If needed, staff will explain why they feel he/she is being dishonest. For example staff might say, "_____ I think you are being dishonest right now because I saw what happened. This is your opportunity to tell me the truth."

(2)   If _____ continues to make false statements, staff will say they cannot listen when he/she is being dishonest and he/she should drop the subject. Staff will pay no additional attention to _____ while continuing the story or perseverating about the issue.

(3)   When/if _____ stops making false statements staff will immediately reinforce the change in behavior by providing immediate attention to him/her. Staff will either start a new conversation with _____ one on one or engage in a preferred activity with him/her.

(4)   If _____ persists with the false statement, staff will continue paying no additional attention to him/her. Staff will tell _____ they cannot listen when the stories are inaccurate. Staff will return several minutes later and begin talking with _____ again asking if he/she would like to tell them what really happened or what is bothering him/her. Staff will tell _____ they appreciate it when he/she is telling the truth. Staff will remind _____ it makes it easier for them to believe him/her when telling the truth.

(5)   Staff will never accuse _____ of lying. Staff will always attempt to verify any statement that _____ makes or story that is told. Staff will remind _____ to be careful with what he/she says. Staff will remind _____ he/she needs to tell the truth if he/she wants other people to believe and trust him/her.

(6)   If _____'s story is accurate, and involves abuse, staff will immediately report this abuse to the appropriate agencies. They will also immediately notify the facility licensee.

(7)   Staff will always carefully attempt to verify any statements or accusations that _____ makes about someone else. Staff will also write down each accusation that _____ makes about someone and their attempts to verify the statements.

INAPPROPRIATE SEXUAL/SOCIAL BEHAVIOR

Definition of the Behavior

Inappropriate sexual/social behavior is defined as _____ attempting to or actually masturbating in public or in a shared room, attempting to touch the genitals of peers, or attempting to assist a peer with masturbation.

*Count as a separate episode every time there is a separate action or attempt made on himself or a peer.

Support Plan

(1)   Because this behavior is often directed at a peer, staff will keep _____ in their direct line of sight at all times. If _____ is wandering around the facility staff will constantly supervise his/her interactions with others especially if in a peer's bedroom or attempting to disengage from the rest of the group.

(2)   Staff will attempt to periodically talk to _____ to ensure that he/she is receiving enough attention and is in a positive emotional state. Staff will ask _____ from time to time if he/she would like to talk with them or engage in an activity. Whenever possible, staff will provide several choices between activities. Staff to occasionally check in with _____ and ask how he/she is feeling. Staff will give _____ an opportunity to talk with them one on one. Staff should always make _____ aware of the amount of time they have, so that _____ is not provoked by staff's inability to spend large amounts of time one on one.

(3)   Staff will remind_____ that everyone has their own personal space and they require it in order to feel comfortable. Through staff explanation, and ongoing conversations from time to time. Staff should physically show _____ how much space they need in order to feel comfortable. Staff will do this by extending their arm outstretched and point to their fingertips saying, "_____ remember to allow others at least this much space when you are interacting with them."

(4)   Staff should discuss with _____ that others do not appreciate when he/she tries to touch them inappropriately. Staff will remind _____ of ways in which he/she can appropriately get the attention of others. For example, staff might say, "_____ to get their attention you should say, excuse me, or hello. I am _____. Would you like to hang out with me?" Staff will remind _____ that this is his/her opportunity to work on him/herself and the way he/she approaches others.

(5)   Staff will have ongoing conversations with _____ that involve why masturbating in a public or shared room is not appropriate and that he/she should do this in privacy. Staff will remind _____ to simply ask for privacy or go into the restroom for privacy. Staff will remind _____ that it is never appropriate to assist a peer in masturbation no matter what room he/she is in and that he/she should never go into a restroom while someone else is using it.

(6)   Staff will verbally praise _____ when allowing an
    appropriate distance between him/herself and another during
    conversations or participating in activities. Staff will say,
    "Good job _____. I appreciate that you allowed that
    person enough space to feel comfortable interacting with you."

(7)   Staff will not rudely deny _____ appropriate
    physical contact.

(8)   Staff will engage _____ in physical activity daily
    for at least 15 minutes to a half hour. This might include going
    on a walk, bouncing a basketball with staff or range of motion
    exercises.

(9)   Whenever staff are creating an activity schedule or
    engaging _____ in an activity they should attempt to
    keep both his/her mind and hands busy and focused on the
    activity by asking questions, co-engaging in the activity, and
    giving him/her objects/pieces to hold on to.

Intervention Plan

(1)   If _____ begins to violate someone's personal space
staff will immediately ask him/her to back up and give the person
some space. At this time, staff will remind _____ to extend
his/her arm outstretched to double check the space being allowed.
_____ will be praised verbally for following the staff's
prompts when he/she allows for personal space or backs up after
being prompted to do so.

(2)   If _____ continues to violate someone's personal
space and is attempting to touch someone inappropriately or
assisting with masturbation. Staff will immediately prompt
_____ to stop. Staff will create space between _____
and the individual and prompt _____ to keep his/her hands
to him/herself. Staff will remind _____ this is not

appropriate and it is time to practice allowing others personal space.

(3)   If _____ is touching him/herself or attempting to masturbate in a shared room staff will immediately prompt to stop using a firm voice. Staff will say, "_____ stop, you need to keep your hands off of yourself right now we are in public." Staff will remind _____ that this is not the place to engage in that behavior and to go into the restroom before beginning to masturbate. Staff will remind _____ that not only does this behavior make others uncomfortable but that continuing it in public could have serious consequences. When having this conversation with _____ staff should do their best to make eye contact with him/her.

(4)   Staff should always redirect _____ into another activity after explaining the behavior is inappropriate. This will include _____ washing his/her hands and engaging his/her hands with a busy activity. _____'s are not free to touch him/herself or others. For example, staff might ask _____ to play cards or begin a painting activity.

(5)   If _____ does not stop touching him/herself or another person, staff will softly but physically stop _____ from touching by gently directing his/her hands away from his/her body or his peers. When applicable, staff will prompt others to leave the immediate area, go into another room, or look away for the time being. Staff will also attempt to direct _____ into the restroom.

(6)   If _____ continues to be sexually inappropriate and the behavior becomes overly offensive to others, staff will carefully document each time the behavior seriously offended someone or took place out in the community.

(7)   Staff will indicate all of the following:

Date and time that the dangerous behavior occurred.

A description of _____'s behavior that required serious intervention to stop   injury/harassment.

A description of redirection attempted before injury/harassment occurred.

Staff person who had to intervene to prevent injury/harassment.

Staff person witnessing the intervention.

(8)   Once _____ has been calm and not sexually aggressive, for 10 minutes, staff will try to talk about the incident. Staff will remind _____ he/she cannot touch him/herself inappropriately while at day program or in a public setting. Staff will remind _____ he/she needs to do this in the privacy of a restroom. Staff will remind _____ that it is important to respect other people's level of comfort and personal space and by continuing to disregard that could also result in arrest or jail time. Staff will explain to _____ that it is never appropriate to assist a peer with masturbation.

(9)   Staff will help _____ determine more appropriate things that can be done next time he/she needs physical contact or to be engaged in an activity. For example, staff might determine that a hand shake or a hug is more appropriate. Staff will remind _____ he/she must always have privacy when touching him/herself and that means going into the restroom. Staff will also remind _____ to respect when someone tells him/her "no" or that they feel uncomfortable doing something.

(10)   If _____'s behavior becomes out of control or overly severe in anyway, endangering the safety of peers, staff will call the administrator, the case worker, and the police to help

with the situation. Staff will report this behavior to licensing by method of Special Incident Report.

If there are any questions regarding these Behavior Support Plans please contact:

Name and Title
Contact Information

Conclusion

In his book, ***POSITIVE BEHAVIOR SUPPORT PLANS Fill in the Blanks***, author Alexander Van Dorn shares his many years of experience supporting individuals with various disabilities and challenging behaviors. His goal is to provide a foundation to create your own *individualized* Behavior Support Plans addressing various behaviors.

It is a rewarding pursuit when small steps toward success are achieved and an increase in positive behaviors become evident. The ultimate goal is to experience increased communication, positive relationships, improved social skills, and a better quality of life.

Be patient, be consistent, and be prepared to revise and rewrite your plans as progress is achieved and skills are increased. It may be that you will also have to revise your plans because little or no progress has occurred. Teach and share with others while reaping the benefits of knowing you have worked very supportively, patiently, and consistently, to better the lives of others.

About the Author

Born, raised, and educated in New York City, Alexander Van Dorn devoted his 45 year career to supporting individuals with intellectual and physical disabilities of all ages. In his earlier years, Alexander Van Dorn, was instrumental in depopulating state institutions and later developing community homes and programs. He has been active working with the court and school systems advocating for the rights of individuals with disabilities. Recently retired, Alexander Van Dorn, often sits on the bank of the Susquehanna River pondering his long career. He has come to realize the insight and knowledge he has gathered over the years must be shared with others. There will be more to come.

Made in the USA
Coppell, TX
05 March 2025